The Virgin Green Guide

The easy way to save the planet and save £££s

First published in Great Britain in 2007 by
Virgin Books Ltd
Thames Wharf Studios
Rainville Road
London
W6 9HA

A catalogue record for this book is available from the British Library.

ISBN 978 07535 12425

FSC

Mixed Sources
Product group from well-managed
forests and other controlled sources

Cert no. SGS - COC - 2061
www.fsc.org
© 1996 Forest Stewardship Council

Typeset by Phoenix Photosetting, Chatham, Kent

Printed and bound in Great Britain by Clays Ltd, Bungay, Suffolk

CONTENTS

INTRODUCTION

'Green issues' are certainly in the news right now. It's becoming clear that we can't treat our planet the way we have been and expect it to continue supporting us.

The ozone layer is thinning, the climate is in turmoil, and the oil and gas are running out. Gloomy stuff? Well, yes, it's serious. But it's not cause for despair.

We got the world in this state, and we can change it. If everyone made just a few small changes to the way they lived, the drain on our poor planet would be tremendously reduced. And we'd be able to pass on the same kind of world to our children and grandchildren that we ourselves inherited.

Yes, there's a lot of environmental harm that's beyond our control – governments and big businesses have a lot to answer for. But there are an awful lot of us 'ordinary people' out there. And all the little changes we make – like recycling, switching off televisions and using energy-efficient light bulbs – can be multiplied millions of times over, to make a **real difference**.

This book will help you to be a part of that difference. We'll show you how to reduce the impact you have on the environment, both locally and on a global scale. It's easy, it can be fun and, what's more, it can even save you money!

Wake up!

Shocking statistics

- The UK produces more than 434 million tonnes of waste every year – a rate of rubbish production that is enough to fill the Albert Hall in London every two hours.
- Every year UK households throw away almost 30 million tonnes of waste. That's the equivalent of three and a half million double-decker buses, which could make a queue stretching from London to Sydney, Australia and back.
- Each person in the UK throws away around £430 worth of food a year.
- The average person in the UK throws away seven times their own body weight in rubbish every year.

Ditch the plastic

- Every year, an estimated 17 billion plastic carrier bags are given away by supermarkets; this is equivalent to over 290 bags for every person in the UK. Fortunately, most supermarkets are introducing schemes to cut down on plastic bag use.
- We produce and use 20 times more plastic today than we did 50 years ago.

Nasty nappies

- Babies' disposable nappies make up about 2 to 4 per cent of the average household rubbish bin. This amounts to 400,000 tonnes of nappy waste sent to landfill sites each year.
- Dealing with nappy waste costs individual local authorities hundreds of thousands of pounds a year.

- In the UK we throw away over eight million disposable nappies each day.

Terrible traffic

- People in the UK make more use of cars than any other European country, despite having below-average car ownership. (Source: CfIT 2001)
- 70 per cent of households in urban areas have at least one car, compared with around 85 per cent of households in rural areas.
- 20,000 hectares of land were changed to transport use from previously undeveloped land between 1985 and 2002. This is roughly equivalent to an area three times the size of the urban area of Nottingham. (Source: DfT Transport Trends 2002)

Paper panic

- Paper and cardboard makes up about one fifth of the contents of household dustbins in the UK, and half of this comes from newspapers and magazines. This is equivalent to over 4kg of waste paper per household in the UK each week that could have been recycled.

Smashing glass

- Glass is just about impossible to break down naturally – it's so long-lasting that ancient glass made many thousands of years ago can still be found in archaeological sites today.
- Recycling two glass bottles will save enough energy to boil water for five cups of tea.

What are we doing wrong?

Slowly but surely, we're swamping the planet with waste – it's everywhere. And we can't blame our overflowing bins and burgeoning landfill sites on 'rubbish gremlins' – it's no one's fault but ours.

It's true that our lives are becoming more and more hectic. We're 'time-poor', and wish we could cram more than 24 hours into the day. And this is where the cult of 'convenience' comes to our rescue. Oh, the joys of disposable pens and razors, and single-serving ready-meals!

But, all too often, with convenience comes an increase in energy consumption, and yet more waste production.

It's time for a drastic rethink of the way we live. Making simple changes is good for the health of the planet, as well as the health of our families. And what's more, it's good for the health of our bank balances as well!

Also, small-scale changes to minimise waste at home add up to minimise waste disposal charges on local communities. And who foots the bill for the rubbish they have to get rid of? Yes, that's right – it's us! So you can see that it's in everyone's best interests to cut down on the amount we consume and throw away.

What about industry?

Some people say, 'It's not my fault – most of the waste and pollution comes from industry.'

It's true that power stations, factories and the like churn out tonnes and tonnes of pollution, but ask yourself who are they making all that power and all those products for? Yes, for you and me.

The more energy and goods we use and demand, the more industry will produce. Certainly, we can lobby government, industry and the big companies to switch to more energy-efficient and environmentally friendly processes, but in the end it's us – the UK population, ever hungry for more energy and 'stuff' – who are demanding the things they produce.

Before the beginning of the twentieth century, 'convenience' wasn't really important to many people. Unless you were very rich, all you wanted to do was get by in relative comfort.

Then, with the 1900s, bigger and bigger factories started churning out a whole range of products designed to make our lives easier. And we liked what we saw! As the years passed, more and more of us bought in to this 'luxury', consumerist lifestyle. Suddenly, it wasn't enough to simply 'get by'. We wanted to fill our homes with TVs, computers, entertainment systems, games consoles, washing machines, spin-dryers and kitchen gadgets, from cappuccino makers to electric juicers. We even want to carry our entertainment with us, with camera-phones and MP3 players – all complete with Bluetooth technology of course!

And it's not enough simply to have these things. We need the latest model if we're to keep up with the Joneses. Even schoolchildren face a rough time in the playground if their mobile phone is last year's model.

Thanks to this constant obsession with being 'up to date', we replace all these 'essential' household appliances and gadgets at a truly alarming rate, with brand-spanking-new, top-of-the-range versions. And what happens to yesterday's technology? That's right, millions of tonnes of yesterday's technology end up as waste.

Now for the 'ecology bit'

It's hard to turn on the TV or radio, or pick up a newspaper without the environment, pollution or climate change making the headlines.

We in the UK gained a comical reputation for always talking about the weather, when in fact we were blessed with a rather mild climate – mild summers and winters and moderate rainfall and winds. In fact, the British weather was really rather boring!

But over the past few decades, things have changed. The climate – both in this country and also on a global scale – seems to be rapidly getting out of hand, with abnormal weather conditions making headline news.

For centuries Britain was blessed with its gentle, temperate climate, but now our weather is becoming increasingly unpredictable, with seven out of the ten warmest years on record occurring in the last decade.

Climate change is nothing new. But throughout history it has been driven by natural events and processes. In more recent times, however – since the industrial revolution – we have been pumping more harmful gases into the Earth's atmosphere as a result of burning fossil fuels. Scientists now believe that the gases produced by burning fossil fuels cause too much heat to be trapped in the atmosphere. And this leads to global warming.

If you're fed up with our chilly winters and our summers that aren't a patch on those in Spain, that may sound like great news! Wouldn't it be great to be able to sunbathe all year round?

Unfortunately, global warming is far from being good news – for anyone.

It's our fault – and we can change it

Our modern lifestyles are possible only thanks to the consumption of immense amounts of energy. Most of the energy we use in our homes is in the form of electricity, and this energy comes largely from fossil fuels such as coal, oil and gas – which are the main fuels used to generate electricity.

We need electricity to keep our homes light, warm and cosy, to keep our food cool and fresh, and cook it, and to power a whole host of other appliances that make our lives easier and more convenient.

No one wants to go back to the Dark Ages. The only problem is that as we demand more and more electricity – and therefore use more fossil fuels – we are pumping more pollution into the atmosphere, causing problems such as global warming and acid rain.

It's time for us to get serious, and cut down on the amount of energy we use.

The Doomsday scenario

Even the boffins can't agree on the full and exact impact global warming will have on our lives – for years there was a big debate on whether humans were actually to blame for it at all!

But it's now clear that it *is* the fault of humans; we now have growing evidence from scientists that it is a very real and serious problem.

Experts have predicted:

- More and more extreme and unpredictable weather conditions. Heavy downpours in the UK now contribute twice as much rain as they did in the early 1960s. Think of the increase in the amount of flooding we get in the UK these days.
- More dangerous and destructive weather on a worldwide scale, such as the disastrous floods and mudslips that devastate huge areas of tropical countries.
- Increased air pollution that will result in more breathing problems such as asthma.
- Changes in the distribution of insects such as mosquitoes. This will lead to the spread of diseases to countries where they were previously unknown.
- Changes in soil quality caused by climate change, compounded by water shortages, which will affect our ability to grow particular types of crops. This will have a knock-on effect on the type and price of food we buy and eat.
- Global warming will cause the Antarctic and Arctic ice sheets to melt, raising sea levels around the world. Scientists from the Intergovernmental Panel on Climate Change (IPCC) estimate that the global average sea level will rise between 0.3 and 2.9 feet (0.09 to 0.88 metres) over the next century. Tropical islands are already being inundated by the sea, and there are fears that whole island communities will be forced to relocate to other countries, leaving their homes and traditional way of life behind.
- By 2010, twenty out of thirty of the world's mega-cities will be on the coast, and therefore threatened by rises in sea level. We only need to look at the devastation caused in the area of New Orleans, to see

what can happen when the climate goes haywire and water levels rise out of control.

> ## Global warming is a killer
> United Nations scientists predict that higher temperatures in Britain over the next 50 years may cause 10,000 more cases of food poisoning, 3,000 extra deaths annually from heatstroke, an extra 5,000 deaths from skin cancer, and 2,000 more cataract operations each year.

What you can do

First of all, you need to learn the 3 Rs.

- REDUCE
- REUSE
- RECYCLE

Your first step is to follow these three simple lifestyle rules. A massive 80 per cent of all household waste can be reduced, reused or recycled. This is your new mantra for a less wasteful lifestyle.

We live in an amazingly wasteful society, but by reducing the amount of 'stuff' we consume, reusing it wherever possible and recycling our rubbish into more useful items, we can protect the environment and save raw materials, energy, space – and the money in our own pockets.

❶ Reduce

We need to cut the amount of waste we produce.

● Look for energy-efficient appliances when buying new electrical items.

● Buy products that will last – both in terms of appliances and clothes.

● Look after your possessions and maintain them well – this will maximise their lifespan.

● Buy 'loose' products at the supermarket to cut down on packaging.

● Donate your old magazines to doctors', dentists', hospitals' and vets' waiting rooms.

● Buy concentrated products, which use less packaging.

❷ Reuse

We can further cut down the waste we produce by buying reusable rather than 'throwaway' products, and reusing certain items – you'll find plenty of advice in this book.

❸ Recycle

● If your local authority collects recyclable materials (e.g. paper, glass) as part of its waste collection service, then take advantage.

● If you can't have your recyclable waste collected, find out where the nearest recycling points are.

● Take old clothes and books to charity shops – it will give you a warm, fuzzy feeling.

● Have a car-boot sale if you want to earn yourself some pocket money.

● Donate old computer and audio-visual equipment to community groups or schools.

What kind of waster are you?

There are many types of waster and we're all guilty of wasting to some extent.

Tick any description from the following list that applies to you and see what your potential saving could be.

TOSSERS

Do you throw out endless binloads of rubbish without a second thought? If so, you're a tosser! What about all that stuff that could be reduced, reused or recycled? Even if you know your 3Rs, you never apply them.

GUZZLERS

Guzzlers are the big energy wasters. You leave lights blazing away in unoccupied rooms, you've got a glut of kitchen and other household electrical gadgets and run them all day long, and when your TV and video aren't switched on, they're on constant stand-by.

BELCHERS

Belchers are the car users, and major polluters in the process. You may even have more than one car and you'd never, ever walk anywhere, let alone think about what damage your fuel is causing.

PLONKERS

Plonkers are large families producing massive overflowing nappy mountains, munching their way through packets and packets of processed food, and binning large quantities of plastic and polystyrene take-away packaging.

SCRAPPERS

Hey, big spenders! If you can't resist buying the latest trendy new clothes, make-up or shoes, then you're a Scrapper. I bet you never wear or use half the stuff you buy and once the latest TV 'fashion guru' tells you it's no longer hip, it'll go straight in the bin, or waste space cluttering up your wardrobe.

SCORING

0–1

Well done! You care about the planet in the right way and you try to do your bit. You probably recycle your newspapers, try to walk or use public transport rather than the car, and buy organic produce from the super-market. You may well be ready for the next step towards green-ness – which means a potential for further savings. In fact, you could notch up a POTENTIAL SAVING of £1,000.

2–3

You're on the right track, but you tend to make excuses. Perhaps you think it takes too much time to always recycle your magazines, so occasionally you'll throw them in the rubbish bin. And you just can't face not using the car – not even for a day. You may be shocked to discover that your POTENTIAL SAVING could be as much as £2,500 a year.

4–5

You really are the pits in green terms! You're hot-water hogs; energy bandits through and through, and wanton wasters of energy and resources. But if you pay attention and change your horrible habits you could make a POTENTIAL SAVING of £4,000 a year. Just think what you could spend it on instead of chucking it away – which is literally what you're doing by being so wasteful.

Do your bit

The world is facing Big Problems. But don't get discouraged. Taking small actions can really make a difference to the planet.

If you just take on board one or two things from each chapter and practise them on a regular basis, you really will be making a big difference.

TOP FIVE TIPS

1. Wherever possible, try to repair things rather than throw them away.
2. If they have to go because you don't like them any more, try to find them a new home by selling them or donating them to a charity shop.
3. If they have to go because they're 'rubbish', see if they can be recycled.
4. Turn off unnecessary lights and appliances.
5. Buy energy-efficient machines, appliances and light bulbs.

1
Shop for the planet

Sad to say, we've become a nation of shopaholics. Consumerism has run out of control as we buy more products than ever before. We want life to be convenient and easy, so we buy overpackaged food and throwaway gadgets – all of which add to increasingly wasteful lifestyles.

At least 'convenience' purchases are aimed at making our lives simpler, and you have to admit that we all seem to have increasing demands on our time. But these days, people think nothing of buying something because they fancy it rather than because they absolutely need it. 'Fashion' – for everything from trainers to mobile phones – has a lot to answer for. We buy 'the latest thing', then we use it for a while, and toss it away when it's gone out of fashion or the novelty has worn off.

The more you shop, the more you drop

The more we buy, the more we throw away. Buying may be fun, but throwing away is nothing but bad news – for the planet and our pockets.

- Getting rid of rubbish uses energy – more fossil fuels burned to contribute to global warming.
- More waste is sent to landfill – many landfill sites are nearly full to bursting and we're running out of suitable land for new sites.
- When you throw something away, you're probably going to buy a new one. Which means more raw materials and more energy being used to make it.

Rather than contributing to the consumerism crisis, use your purchasing power in a good way. Think about 'precycling' as well as recycling. If you think about what you buy BEFORE you buy it, you can cut down the amount you have to recycle or throw away.

Just think, you could cut your garbage by as much as 20 per cent simply by being more 'shop smart'.

Changing your shopping habits

All of us like to have nice things, right? A growing number of us are using 'retail therapy' to counter our increasingly stressful and busy lives. Shopping can give us an instant 'high' and buying new things makes us feel good. However, for many, these spending habits are becoming increasingly difficult to manage.

Credit is easy to come by and advertisers are hell-bent on encouraging us to borrow more and spend more. That's hardly surprising when you consider that advertising is essentially designed to create demand regardless of whether a product meets the genuine needs of consumers.

It's generally the ladies who are tagged with the label 'shopaholic', but more and more men are now compulsive spenders. And whilst girls tend to buy clothes, shoes, perfume and make-up, the guys are shelling out for all sorts of electronic equipment, sports gear and car accessories – and none of that comes cheap!

Are you a 'shopping slave'?

● Do you buy things you don't need, use or want?
● Are you spending more than you can afford?
If either of these are the case, then you may have a problem.

It's not that we should never go shopping again, just because of the temptation to overindulge and splurge, which we all sometimes give in to. But for 'shopaholics' it's a different matter. They are compulsive spenders who act this way most of the time, not just occasionally.

The only way to reduce waste and improve the environment is to start thinking about what we buy and how often and where we buy it. Remember, this is all about changing our habits and thinking in a different way.

● Buy environment-friendly products.
● Consider having your supermarket shopping delivered. Not only will this save you time and hassle, it will also save fuel. Just think, rather than your car ferrying just you (with maybe your family in tow), a little van will deliver lots of people's shopping in a single round trip.

QUIZ – Are you a shopaholic?

☐ Do you get an instant 'high' when you shop?
☐ Do you head straight for the shops when you're feeling wound-up or miserable?
☐ Do you buy things you already own?
☐ Do you buy things you don't need?
☐ Do you buy clothes or shoes without trying them on?
☐ Do you buy CDs that you never listen to?
☐ Do you have more than one credit card or store card?
☐ Do you often spend up to the limit on your credit cards?
☐ Do you hide things that you buy from your partner, friends or family?
☐ When you've really splashed out on something, do you lie about how much it costs?

If you answer 'yes' to more than five of these questions, your spending may be getting out of control. Try to figure out what triggers your spending sprees. Do you head for the shops if you've had a row with your partner, or had a spat with your boss at work? Or did you see a friend with some new clothes which made you feel that you need an instant image makeover? Are your shopping habits driven by feelings of low self-esteem?

Knowledge is power – once you're aware of why you feel the need to shop and spend, you'll be in a position to do something about it.

The seven deadly sins of shopping

Do you recognise your deadly sin (or sins) from the list below? If you do, follow our advice to become more shopping savvy.

❶ Greed

You have an insatiable desire for designer labels and expensive jewellery and you simply refuse to go for the cheap option. Do you really need 20 handbags in various colours and sizes, 18 pairs of identical trousers, 14 different types of shampoo and conditioner?

You're just greedy for purchases – you're the king and queen of bling! You're driven by fashion's latest fads and you simply have to have the latest model.

>>

>>

And how do you manage to keep on spending so much? Easy, every-thing's bunged straight on to a credit card, so you're probably always in debt.

What should you do? You need to think about reducing, reusing and repairing stuff if you really can't face the thought of buying bargains. When it comes to clothes, you need to learn to be more discerning. You need a capsule wardrobe, rather than an over-flowing closet where you can never find anything. Stick to a few quality basics, in neutral colours that suit you, and that you can mix and match.

Be honest, you really don't need twenty white shirts – just keep the best ones that you simply can't bear to part with and make sure you wear them. Any items of clothing you don't need should be given to friends who will wear them or bagged up and taken to a charity.

❷ Gluttony

The shopping glutton is the typical impulse buyer. When you prowl around the supermarket, you're always alert for a bargain, or some-thing new to try. Which means that you come home with a load of stuff you didn't think you needed before you set out. And, if you're honest, that you didn't really need.

Overdoing it on your supermarket shopping means wasted money and wasted food. Or, if you eat it rather than throwing it away, possible extra inches added to your waistline!

>>

What should you do? Write a shopping list – and stick to it!

❸ Lust

You're an uncontrollable pleasure-seeker and a very high-maintenance guy or gal. If you're a girlie, then we'd find heaps of high heels, handbags and sexy undies at home. And if you're a fella you'll forever be buying 'boy toys' – battery-operated beer openers, games consoles and electronically powered toy cars and other executive toys.

What should you do? You need to get a grip on your spending habits. All this costs money, and buying unnecessary 'stuff' is a drain on the environment in terms of raw materials and energy.

If you really can't curb your lust of the fun things in life, try to buy the best you can and stick to one 'luxury' item per year.

❹ Wrath

If this is you, you just hate sharing, don't you? You're a bit of a squirrel, too, hoarding tonnes of stuff that you never use. But woe betide anyone who pinches a squirt from one of your ten bottles of perfume.

Your wardrobe is a real mix of styles because you buy things on a whim, or to cheer yourself up when you're angry and fed up with the way the world is treating you. You buy things to suit your current mood only to have a hissy fit and consign last week's fave purchase to the darkest recesses of your closet when you see that it makes your bum look big.

What should you do? Every time you buy something new, go through your belongings and give something to charity that you no longer need or like. Your task is to clear the clutter before you even consider getting anything new.

❺ Envy

Your number-one occupation is keeping up with the Joneses. If they've got one, you want one too. A better one, if possible. And if you could only be three stones lighter, then you'd feel much more attractive. But the truth is, it's hard to keep up with the Joneses and trying too hard will only make you miserable.

And stop being too hard on yourself, or imagining that the grass is always greener on the other side of the fence, or that everything will be perfect once you've slimmed down to a size 10.

What should you do? Store all your 'thin' clothes in a bag, label them and set a date of six months. Promise yourself that if you're still not in them by then you'll let them go.

❻ Sloth

Your wardrobe is stacked with stuff from the 1970s that you meant to get rid of, but never quite got around to.

What should you do? You need to sort out your wardrobe NOW! Did you know that 80 per cent of people wear only 20 per cent of the clothes they own? You need to bag them up and take them to a charity shop, or have a clothes-swap party with some friends.

❼ Pride

You want to look fabulous all the time, so you're forever spending a fortune on expensive face creams, make-up and other beauty products to keep yourself in tip-top shape. If you're a bloke, then you're a bit of a Beckham — with a bathroom brimming with 'grooming' products.

While it's good to take pride in your appearance, you can overdo the purchasing in the pursuit of perfection. Limit yourself to the essentials, then treat yourself to just a couple of luxury buys. Ladies, you really do not need fourteen lip-glosses in various fruity flavours.

What should you do? If you buy make-up then ask an assistant at a beauty counter to help you choose what suits your face, age and skin. That way you won't be tempted to buy what you've seen in a magazine in the hope that it'll suit you.

Think about what you love most — if it's designer labels then buy classics that won't date.

>>

> If you buy make-up, make sure the product contains natural and non-harmful ingredients, that it has not been tested on animals, that packaging is kept to an absolute minimum and that the company has an ethical policy towards its workers and operations.

What to buy
Choose quality

In the long run, it pays to buy high-quality goods that will last. This means that, because more goods don't have to be made to replace the cheaper ones you might have bought (and thrown away – more waste!) the environment will benefit. And what's more, although quality and reusable products may cost a little more now, over time they'll save you money.

Good examples of reusable products include rechargeable batteries, ink pens rather than throwaway ballpoints, and 'proper' razors rather than disposables. Cotton hankies (rather than tissues) and cloth nappies (instead of disposables) may mean extra washing, but in the long run it's kinder to the environment, and cheaper for you.

Buy in bulk

Stock up with non-perishable products such as household cleaners, toilet rolls and kitchen towels in bulk, as you'll only have one container or outer wrapper to throw away. To be even greener, you could make your own cleaning products using 'ingredients' from your kitchen cupboard (see page 142).

Share and share alike

It's a good idea to hire items you don't use often rather than buying them, or you may also be able to borrow them from friends, family and neighbours. Items such as ladders, garden equipment, power tools, party supplies and some sports equipment are just a few things that spring to mind.

And if you've got any items you don't want any more, give them to a friend (who will probably remember the favour and might do the same for you another time), or donate them to charity.

Help a good cause

You can also help charities by buying from their stores – before buying items such as furniture, crockery, linen or clothes, check out the charity shops.

Care for your belongings

Look after your things, and they will serve you well. Especially if you've bought good quality in the first place, you'll find your belongings – from crockery and furniture to bed linen and clothes – will last that much longer.

And if something gets damaged, don't instantly rush out to buy a new one – see if it can be repaired. The Yellow Pages lists repair services for a whole host of household items.

Think outside the box

This is the 'reuse' part of the 'Reduce, Reuse, Recycle' mantra. If you think creatively, you're sure to find ingenious new uses for items that would otherwise end up in the bin. Resealable food containers can be washed thoroughly and used to keep leftovers fresh in the fridge, or used as free lunchboxes. Jam jars can be used to store dry goods such as rice, pasta and lentils.

In fact, containers of all sorts, from all kinds of products, can find a new lease of life with a whole variety of novel uses – plant-pot holders, make-up caddies and pen holders are just a few ideas. If you have children, it's great fun for them to decorate the containers.

And it's not just containers that can find new uses. Old clothes you wouldn't dream of wearing in public can be relegated to 'decorating wear', and old sheets make perfect dust sheets to cover up your furniture.

- If you need something, but won't use it very often, rent rather than buy. Big appliances like garden machinery and carpet cleaners can be wonderfully useful, but do you really need your own? Do your budget – and the environment – a favour and hire one whenever you need to use it. Other good examples are party decorations and crockery – some supermarkets and wine merchants hire out glasses for parties, saving you from buying extra glasses or disposable cups.
- For battery-powered items such as electric toothbrushes, cameras and shavers, buy rechargeable items instead of ones powered by disposable batteries.
- Some eco-friendly cosmetics companies allow you to take their empty bottles and containers back to the shop to be refilled.
- It's trendy to shop in charity shops – take advantage of other people's poor taste, and snap up the perfectly usable (and often rather

fantastic) things they donate. And you'll be helping the charity at the same time, which can't be bad.

Avoid unnecessary chemicals

When buying items such as household cleaning products, washing products, and bathroom staples such as soap, shampoos and cosmetics, go for the most environmentally friendly option. Minimise your reliance on potentially hazardous chemicals. Read the label, and choose brands with good environmental credentials. Or make your own products from what's in the kitchen cupboard (see page 142).

Beware salespeople

It doesn't take a genius to work out that salespeople don't necessarily have our best interests at heart. These guys and girls are professionals, and it's their job to make a profit, by making you think that you just MUST have their product.

Next time you've listened to the sales patter, and are just about to hand over your hard-earned cash for that cosmetics gift set, scarf you can wear thousands of different ways, or even that new car, stop and think. If possible, go away and think about it. Impulse buys are all too often unwise buys.

Remember recycling

Wherever possible, buy recycled and recyclable products.

Learn the symbols that indicate whether a product is made from recycled materials, and whether it can be recycled when you've finished with it. If you do both of these things, you've closed the recycling loop.

A huge variety of household items can be made from recycled materials. For example, look for recycled glass bottles or paper products. You can even get cat litter made from recycled newspaper!

Plastics are harder to recycle, but some companies have managed to do this – though these are generally from companies that specialise in 'green' products.

Jargon buster

The labelling on recycled products can sometimes be confusing.

● Pre-consumer – these products are made with recycled material that came from leftovers in the manufacturing process.
● Post-consumer – this means it's made with recycled material that came from a community recycling programme – 100 per cent post-consumer is the ultimate in recycling.

The great nappy mountain

Every day, people in the UK throw out around eight million disposable nappies. These then get taken to landfill sites, filling up rapidly dwindling space in these underground disposal dumps. And because disposable nappies contain plastic they take ages to break down – up to 500 years in some cases.

The best way to reduce rubbish is to reduce the amount of 'stuff' you consume – and this is true for nappies just as much as other items.

We're not saying that real nappies are squeaky clean when it comes to their environmental image – they still have to be washed, which uses chemicals and energy. But the landfill issue is an important one, and nappies are a substantial contributor to landfill waste.

Many people are put off cloth nappies by the fact that you have to wash them. But reusable nappies have come a long way in recent years. Although the traditional triangular version is still very popular, you can now get self-fastening and specially fitted styles.

And if you really can't bear the thought of all that washing, why not try out one of the many nappy-washing services? Just type 'nappy washing service' into an Internet search engine to find one near you. Or try the website www.wen.org.uk, where you'll find plenty of useful information on cloth nappies, not to mention other green issues, from the Women's Environmental Network.

Money saver

- By using cloth nappies and washing them yourself, you could save around £500 over a child's 'nappy-wearing life'. If you have a second child, the savings mount up, as you already have a stock of nappies.
- A nappy-washing service might cost you around £10 a week – about the same as it would cost you to buy disposable nappies that would end up in a landfill site.

Learning the green claims code

When you're shopping with an eye to the environment, you need to know what you're buying. Everything you buy will have some kind of impact on the environment – through its production, distribution, use and disposal – but you want to choose the products that do the least harm.

But sometimes it's hard to decipher all of the often confusing logos, and sometimes downright misleading claims on the packaging and in product literature.

The government Department for Environment, Food and Rural Affairs (Defra) has produced a Green Claims Code, to help consumers distinguish between products that are genuinely less harmful to the environment and those that make bogus 'green claims'. The Green Claims Code is a voluntary code for manufacturers, which gives guidelines on providing environmental information about a product.

What is a 'green' claim?

A green claim is any information provided about the environmental characteristics of a product. These can be claims made in product literature, adverts and on packaging, and can appear in the form of symbols, text or graphics.

The Code aims to ensure that:

- Claims about the environmental aspects of a product are accurate and informative.
- Self-proclaimed green claims made by manufacturers are not misleading.
- Consumers are able to check the green claims made by manufacturers about their products.

These are examples of fair and accurate green claims:

● 'This paper comprises 80% post-consumer waste'
● 'Paper manufactured using 100% recycled post-consumer waste, collected from recycling banks'
● 'Pencils made from sustainable FSC (Forest Stewardship Council) accredited timber'

These are examples of misleading green claims:

● 'Now contains twice the recycled content'
  What's the problem?
  If the product only contained 5 per cent recycled material to start with, the new version is still only 10 per cent recycled – hardly impressive. If something contains only a small proportion of recycled material, it's misleading to claim that it is 'a recycled product'. If a product is 100 per cent recycled, then it should be stated clearly and in plain language.
● 'Now uses less energy'
  What's the problem?
  If the claim doesn't go on to explain why and how it uses less energy, this is a woolly and unhelpful claim. The Green Claims Code states that any product comparisons need to be qualified. The example above should say something like: 'uses 20% less electricity in normal use than our previous model'.

Beware of ambiguous claims such as 'sustainable' or 'non-polluting' and watch for vague descriptions such as 'friendly', 'kind' and 'safe' being linked with words such as 'Earth', 'nature' and 'environment'.

Companies using their own 'green' symbols or logos

Some companies try to reassure their consumers with apparently 'green' logos, but this is potentially misleading unless it is accompanied by a clear statement, in line with the Green Claims Code, that explains just what the image represents.

Pictures and symbols of globes, trees, flowers, the sun, etc. shouldn't be used unless there is a direct link between the product, the object and the environmental benefit that the company is claiming.

For example, the 'never-ending' Möbius loop is probably the most familiar green symbol, and if it is used for claims of recycled content, the percentage of recycled content should be clearly stated.

Complaints about green claims

If you think the manufacturer is trying to pull the wool over your eyes, or you're simply baffled by green claims on a product, you should contact the head office of the manufacturer (or retailer if it's their own brand) and ask for an explanation of the claim and how it complies with the Green Claims Code.

If you think the claim is simply untrue, or you're not satisfied with the explanation given by the manufacturer or retailer, speak to your local authority trading standards department. Give them details of the claim and any other relevant information you have.

Complaints about a claim on radio or TV can be made to Ofcom. If the material is printed or is on the Internet contact the Advertising Standards Authority.

Let the web do the work

Shopping online is a growing trend in this country.

Shopping by mouse can:

- Save you time.
- Save you money through buying in bulk.
- Cut down on traffic pollution thanks to fewer car journeys to out-of-town shopping centres and supermarkets.
- Allow you to find out more about a company and its products, through its website.
- Help you to make more informed choices. By using shopping comparison websites you can look at product reviews and rating systems so you can read comments from other purchasers and make comparisons between various products.
- Enable you to shop at a time that's convenient for you, rather than having to fit in with shop opening times.

Online shopping is also good for elderly people or those who have trouble accessing shopping centres because transport isn't readily available.

Home delivery

Home delivery services are becoming ever more popular, and with good reason – we're working longer hours and leading increasingly busy lives. Supermarket delivery services save fuel (and your time), but even better is a local organic vegetable and fruit box that comes with minimum packaging.

Townies as well as country folk can benefit from organic deliveries. If you're a busy Londoner, for instance, the Organic Delivery Company can bring all sorts of organic goodies straight to your front door. Delivery is free for orders of £13.95 and above and you can set up a regular order (either online or by phone) or just have a one-off delivery.

Visit www.organicdelivery.co.uk to order.

There are lots of local delivery services and box schemes to choose from. Local box schemes consist of a box of organic foods which come straight from the growers and are packed and delivered to your home – so there are no middlemen and no shops involved, and you know you're doing your bit to support the local economy. You also know your food hasn't had to be flown halfway around the world before it arrives on your plate.

Visit the Soil Association's website, www.soilassociation.org, which has a list of organic producers and suppliers.

Check out these online links

If you really want to see purchasing power in action, then look no further than Ethical Consumer (www.ethicalconsumer.org). This organisation turns the spotlight on some of the major achievements brought about by consumer pressure over the years, and has information on all the latest consumer boycotts.

Alternatively, you can subscribe to Ethical Consumer's Ethiscore website. This contains over 110 reports, with company information that's updated daily so you get the most accurate ethical information possible. At the time of publication it cost £15 to subscribe for a year.

If you would like to know more about the issues surrounding your purchases, you could also check out www.greenchoices.org, which has links to some of the best ethical companies and organisations on the web, selling everything from food to holidays.

For one-stop ethical shopping there's The Green Shop, which offers a mail-order service through www.greenshop.co.uk. It stocks a range of essentials of its own and many well-known ethical brands.

You'll find a hugely extensive one-stop ethical shop online through the Natural Collection catalogue at www.naturalcollection.com, a trading partner for Friends of the Earth.

The Centre for Alternative Technology's website, www.cat.org.uk, is perfect for those of you who wish to take your 'green' credentials one step further. It lists courses and books on how to make your life more sustainable, and a range of energy-saving products such as radiator insulator panels and solar battery rechargers.

In our world of disposable nappies, plastic bottles and PVC toys, it can be hard for today's mums to find eco-friendly baby products. Help is at hand, though, from www.greenbabyco.com.

Shop smart for food

A family of four will waste an average of £5,160 a year. It's a shocking waste, not just in terms of money down the drain, but also on moral grounds, don't you think? When people around the world are starving, it seems unethical to buy fresh food 'just in case we need it, so that it ends up mouldering away, and eventually chucked in the bin.

It only takes a bit of discipline and planning to change things. Sit down at the beginning of the week and plan your meals. You don't need to chart them in minute detail, just enough to know what you need to buy.

Not only will you save money and avoid waste, you'll also feel calmer once you don't have a mad scramble at the last minute as you frantically dash around the kitchen trying to figure out what you can make from all the stuff in your fridge and your cupboards!

Yes, everyone gets it wrong sometimes. We've all found the occasional mouldy vegetable lurking at the back of the fridge, or bought too much fresh milk because we didn't realise we were going to be out so much that week. But if you plan your food shopping rather than wandering around the supermarket like a child in a sweet shop, the planet – as well as your wallet – will thank you for it. And, probably, your sense of calm and your waistline will as well! Calm, sensible, organised cooking is better for your health.

Do you really need it?

Super-saver deals, buy-one-get-one-free, three-for-twos and special offers. Every time we set foot in the supermarket or hit the high street, we're bombarded by advertising. The marketing guys and girls want to convince us they're doing us a favour, and helping us to save money. Sometimes they are – canny shoppers can save money, and waste, by taking advantage of **the right** special offers.

Buying things like washing powder and toilet rolls in bulk saves both money and packaging. And taking advantage of special offers on things like shampoo and toothpaste, things that last for ages, is a good idea too. But, especially when it comes to food items, you have to watch the shelf life. If you are buying dry goods, such as breakfast cereal, flour, or the 'biscuit' kind of pet food, it makes good sense to buy the larger, more economical size – but only if you know you'll use it all up before the 'use by' date.

Perishable goods can be a minefield when it comes to avoiding waste. Only take advantage of special offers if you know you're going to use it all in time. Is a double-sized carton of orange juice for only one-and-a-half times the price really such a great deal, if you're never going to finish it in time? And a special 'economy pack' of twelve yogurts may be a great idea if you have a family who all take one to school or work in their lunchboxes. But otherwise, you could end up throwing half of them away.

The perils of packaging

Overpackaging means that we're literally returning home with bags full of rubbish every time we go shopping. Next time you shop, take a good long look at what's in your basket. How much of that is packaging? How much is really necessary?

And remember, the cost of packaging is included in the price of each product, and passed on to us, so essentially we're paying for rubbish. In fact, packaging can cost as much as 16p in every pound of your purchase. Which means that when you buy an item costing £2.00, you could be paying 32p for the privilege of carrying home and throwing away the packaging that comes with it.

Yes, some packaging is necessary, to keep food fresh, or protect things from being crushed. But a lot of packaging is clearly just for decoration, or simply a gimmick. Think of all those 'lunchbox' foods aimed at children. Does your child really need cheese cut into funny shapes and individually wrapped, or snack-size boxes of raisins? What's wrong with slicing a big wedge of cheese into matchbox sized pieces, or putting some raisins in a reusable tub?

So, always look for the product with the least packaging, and avoid multilayered products. Anything with loads of excessive packaging means that you're literally throwing money away!

Buying fresh fruit and vegetables is one area where you can really save on packaging – or alternatively, get it badly wrong.

- Always try to buy 'loose' rather than pre-packed fruit and veg.
- Buy fruit and vegetables in season wherever possible. Admittedly, if you want a pineapple, it's going to have come from overseas. But do we really need tomatoes from Israel, apples from New Zealand or lettuces from Spain? Think of the fuel that's used to fly your fruit and veg halfway across the planet!

Bags of trouble

Plastic bags are an ecological nightmare – when taken to landfill sites, they can take 200 years to break down. Many supermarkets are trying to discourage their use, and offering bag-recycling schemes.

Do your bit to reduce plastic bag waste by:

- Buying a tough supermarket 'bag for life', rather than using the flimsy free bags available from the checkout, and reuse it until it needs replacing. Supermarkets will usually replace their own bags for life for free.
- Bring your own shopping bag. If you want to be really green, make your own, or buy an unbleached hessian one from a 'green' stockist.

Supermarket check list

As you walk out of the supermarket, think about your purchases, and do our simple check list in your head. How good do you feel about it?

Try to minimise the amount of packaging you carry home. Aim for one layer of packaging – max! If you're bringing home more than four things in each category below, you're bringing home way too much!

❑ Plastic supermarket carrier bags
❑ Cardboard packaging with more packaging inside
❑ Unnecessary plastic wrapping materials
❑ Plastic bottles
❑ Items with polystyrene packaging

Top supermarket tips

Top tips for low-waste supermarket shopping:

● Make a list and stick to it – only buy what you need and try to resist those special offers if they don't represent a true saving.

● Buy fruit and vegetables loose rather than pre-packaged. Not only does it cut down on packaging that harms the environment, it's also cheaper – why should you have to pay for plastic?

● Choose glass bottles, or tins over plastic packaging that can be difficult and expensive to recycle.

● Buy reusable goods that last longer than single-use disposable versions of products such as razors, pens and nappies.

● Avoid using the free plastic bags by taking your own shopping bag.

● Save on time and petrol by using the supermarket recycling banks whenever you shop.

● Buy concentrated versions of washing liquid, washing-up liquid, and fabric softener, to save on packaging. You might save money, too.

Choosing organic

The Soil Association mark guarantees that the product is organic, and can be found on a whole host of goods. Organic farming does not use chemical fertilisers and pesticides, which benefits the soil, the food, and the environment, so it's good to go organic if you can. It may cost a bit more, but you'll have the peace of mind of knowing it hasn't been sprayed with chemicals. Organic food often tastes far better and scientists believe that some organic foods are higher in nutrients than non-organic foods.

Meat

If you're a meat eater then try to buy organic or free range. These animals will have been reared under more natural conditions with less (or no) artificial hormones or pesticides. That means it's much better for you (you're eating fewer chemicals and drugs), better for the environment, and for the animal's welfare when it was alive! Organic meat can be expensive though, so why not eat a vegetarian meal a few nights a week and then splash out on an organic steak for the weekend? You'll save money, and your waistline will thank you too, as healthy vegetarian foods are lower in fat than meat.

Fish

The Marine Stewardship Council sets an internationally recognised standard to measure and reward sustainably managed fisheries.

Make it Fairtrade

When you're next buying coffee, tea, chocolate and other imported goods such as nuts or dried fruit, look for the Fairtrade logo. Fairtrade ensures that small farmers in developing countries receive a fair share of the money you pay for their product.

Farmers' markets

Farmers' markets have boomed in popularity and number in recent years and there are now over 500 held around the country. All the food is locally produced, generally unpackaged and usually grown by the person selling it to you.

Advantages of farmers markets:

- Buying direct from the farmer who has grown or reared the produce means that you know where your food has come from, and can ask about how the food was grown or how the animals were reared.
- You're doing your bit to support the UK's farmers, and your local economy.
- You're reducing your shopping basket's 'food miles'.

To find your nearest farmer's market visit www.farmersmarkets.net for a full list. If there isn't one locally, you may be lucky enough to have a farm shop nearby.

City dwellers don't have to miss out on fresh farm food, either. There are a number of city farms operating in a similar way. Visit www.farm-garden.org.uk to find your nearest one.

Wood

When you are buying wood products check for the Forest Stewardship Council (FSC) mark.

In order to use that mark, a company has to use sustainable timber harvested from a well-managed forest.

Another 'green' alternative is to buy reclaimed timber, which is fully seasoned and lacks the 'raw' look of new wood.

Paints

Many types of paints and solvents contain 'volatile organic compounds' (VOCs). These cause air pollution and are hazardous to your health, so buy low or VOC-free paints wherever possible. There are several suppliers of environmentally friendly paint – even one made from clay that, believe it or not, requires only one coat, is quick to dry and comes in a lovely range of shades. For eco-friendly paints try The Green Shop at www.greenshop.co.uk.

Clothes

Now I know that in the past 'vegetarian' shoes looked as if you were wearing loaves of bread on your feet, but things have come a long way since then! So, if you really want to wear your green credentials on your sleeve then look no further than www.greenfibres.com, which sells clothes made from organic fabrics. Try www.hug.co.uk for a range of cotton clothing, including some especially cute baby wear.

Hemp is about as green as a fibre can be, as it grows without the need for pesticides and is biodegradable. Check out www.motherhemp.com for more details.

Shopping with the seasons

Of course it would be lovely to eat strawberries all year round — and now we can, if we're prepared to pay. But have you ever stopped to think about where the food you buy comes from? That strawberry that you're munching outside its usual summer season may have been flown in from Spain or even further afield.

Those air miles clocked up by your food aren't good news for the environment. Why? It's simple. It takes enormous quantities of fuel to transport the food, and therefore large amounts of damaging carbon dioxide are released into the atmosphere, contributing to global warming. And who foots the bill for this ecological scandal? Would it surprise you to learn it was you? Somebody has to pay for that transportation, so that's another hidden cost that doesn't appear on your shopping bill.

You can do your bit by simply stopping to think about where your food comes from, and making the right choices — it can make a world of difference.

Base your meals around these seasonal crops, to avoid unnecessary air miles in your shopping basket. And remember to check that your fruit and veg have indeed come from this country. All too often, as you browse the supermarket shelves, you'll find produce that could have been grown in the UK, but has actually been flown in from overseas.

Spring

- Asparagus
- Broccoli
- Brussels sprouts
- Carrots
- Leeks
- Lettuce
- Parsnips
- Radishes
- Spinach
- Spring cabbage
- Spring onions
- Strawberries
- Tomatoes
- Turnips
- Winter cabbage

Summer

- Asparagus
- Aubergine
- Beetroot
- Broad beans
- Carrots
- Cauliflower
- Courgettes
- Cucumber
- French beans
- Lettuce
- Mangetout
- Onions
- Peas
- Potatoes
- Radishes
- Runner beans
- Spinach
- Spring onions
- Summer cabbage
- Sweet corn
- Tomatoes
- Turnips

Autumn

- Apples
- Blackberries
- Blackcurrants
- Cherries
- Cooking apples
- Dessert apples
- Gooseberries
- Onions
- Peaches
- Pears
- Plums
- Potatoes

Winter

- Aubergine
- Beetroot
- Brussels sprouts
- Carrots
- Cauliflower
- Celery
- Cucumber
- French beans
- Leeks
- Lettuce
- Onions
- Parsnips
- Peas
- Potatoes
- Radishes
- Red cabbage
- Runner beans
- Swede
- Sweet corn
- Turnips
- Winter cabbage

Remember, beauty comes from within, so don't make the planet suffer just so that you can look good.

What you have saved ...

You've done this ...	Result
Saved £430 worth of food a year from being a more conscious consumer and not buying food that never gets eaten	Avoided wasting food and money
Bought from small local shops, buying fresher (hopefully organic) goods with less packaging	Supported the local economy, reduced the amount of pesticides used, and reduced the amount of packaging produced (that has to be disposed of)
Bought products that last, such as cotton hankies and energy-saving light bulbs	Saved raw materials and energy – as well as the cash in your wallet

Case Study
The Tibbett family

Marianne and John and their four daughters: Catherine aged 2, Genevieve (4), Francesca (6) and Annabel (8).

The Tibbetts were throwing away about 20 bags of rubbish every week. When the family were asked to tip 17 bags of their waste out in their back garden and sort through it, it turned out that they were throwing out huge amounts of food. In fact, 20 per cent of their rubbish was food waste.

Lessons for the Tibbetts:

Their local authority actually had one of the best recycling rates in the country (39 per cent) and they as a family were letting the side down.

They would soon have a doorstep recycling scheme put into place, so they needed to learn how to separate their rubbish anyway.

The Tibbetts learned their 3 Rs – reduce, reuse, recycle – and soon managed to get their landfill waste down to three bags. With practice and reduction of packaging, they resolved to reduce it even further.

The Tibbetts' main waste problem was that huge amount of food they were throwing away. Their food waste nearly filled a wheelbarrow and apart from the fact they were wasting a huge amount of money, they had been sending it to landfill, which was resulting in methane being produced as it broke down.

We eat huge amounts of meat and therefore have millions of ruminants roaming the Earth eating grass, farting and producing methane – a notorious greenhouse gas. Their poo also produces huge amounts of nitrogen that pollutes water sources. The Tibbetts did not want to become vegetarians, but were prepared to cut down on the number of meat-based meals – to save money and waste.

They were lucky enough to have a good-sized garden, which opened up a fantastic eco-opportunity to them – chickens! There's a company called Omlet who supply chickens complete with their own 'eglu', which has to be the most stylish and innovative chicken house ever. It is a great way to keep chickens as pets and, because of its clever design, you can have fresh eggs whether you live in the country, city or suburbs. Find out more at www.omlet.co.uk. Chickens only cost 3p a day to keep and a pair can produce up to a dozen eggs a week. It's probably one of the most sustainable ways for a family to produce their own protein.

The Tibbetts were delighted with the new additions to their family. In fact, little Genevieve said, 'Do you know who my best friends are? The chickens. I love them already!' This was an hour after their arrival.

Not only were the kids delighted with 'Chicken Licken' and 'Henny Penny', but the new additions could eat all the family's veggie waste.

Shocking statistics

● The UK creates enough packaging debris a year – an amazing 9 million tonnes –to fill 13,000 jumbo jets.

● On average, a UK family consumes around 330 glass bottles and jars a year (source: British Glass).

● The UK produces and uses around 20 times more plastic than it did 50 years ago (source: Waste Watch).

USEFUL CONTACTS:

Advertising Standards Authority (www.asa.org.uk, telephone 020 7492 2222, Advertising Standards Authority, Mid City Place, 71 High Holborn, London WC1V 6QT) for if you want to complain about an advert in print or on the Internet. **Ofcom** (www.ofcom.org.uk) if you want to complain about an advert on the TV or radio.

Centre for Alternative Technology (www.cat.org.uk) for green information and courses.

The Confederation of City farms and Community Gardens (www.farmgarden.org.uk) is the representative body for city farms, community gardens and similar community-led organisations in the UK.

Eglu (www.omlet.co.uk) for innovative chicken housing.

Ethical Consumer (www.ethicalconsumer.org) is the UK's leading alternative consumer organisation.

Farmers Markets (www.farmersmarkets.net) has information on farmers' markets.

Green Baby (www.greenbabyco.com) for eco-friendly baby products.

Green Choices (www.greenchoices.org) has links to ethical organisations on the web.

Natural Collection catalogue (www.naturalcollection.com), a trading partner for Friends of the Earth.

The Green Shop (www.greenshop.co.uk) for mail order ethical products.

2
High energy

A waste of energy

Wasted energy is invisible, but it's one of the worst environmental problems there is. During the golden years of gas and oil exploration in the UK we were self-sufficient in gas and even exported it. It's a sobering thought that within the next twenty years we could be importing up to 80 per cent of our gas from places as far flung as Russia and Malaysia.

If we think gas is expensive now, what will it cost then?

Almost all the energy we use comes from fossil fuels (oil, gas and coal) and burning these releases harmful gases like carbon dioxide and sulphur dioxide into the atmosphere. Carbon dioxide, in turn, contributes to the greenhouse effect and causes changes in our climate, while sulphur dioxide creates sulphuric acid and adds to the problem of acid rain.

The energy we use to heat and power our homes is responsible for just over a quarter of the UK's carbon dioxide emissions, making us a big contributor to environmental damage.

So, how can we reduce energy waste in the home? We need to reduce the amount of energy we consume, and make the most efficient use of the energy we do use, so that we cut our monthly fuel bills but still retain the same level of comfort we're used to now.

When we're energy efficient in terms of the way we power, heat and light our homes, we reduce our energy requirements and reduce our reliance on power stations. That has the knock-on effect of cutting down our contribution to climate change and other forms of environmental damage.

There are plenty of ways you can save energy in the home, and many of them will mean huge savings on your fuel bills too.

The first step is to find out where you're going wrong, and where you can reduce the amount of power you consume, leading to:

- Less waste
- Less environmental damage
- More money in your pocket

Like any lifestyle overhaul, some of the actions we'll be recommending require a bit of thought, and dedication. But once you've made an effort for a few weeks, you'll find the changes that seemed such an effort at first have become second nature and you don't even have to think about them.

Some of the measures we suggest may mean a bit of extra expenditure – but in the long run, you'll be saving. Being energy efficient can be one of the biggest money-savers in the home and, if you're not convinced after following the advice in this book, just you wait until you get your next fuel bill!

Remember, nothing in this book is about deprivation or going without everything that makes life pleasant. It's simply about making sensible and more responsible choices.

Shock statistic!
The British public wastes around £5 billion worth of energy a year.

Home energy audit
You need to figure out how much energy you actually consume – and where you might be wasting it. Once you have an overall picture of where the biggest areas of waste are, you can set to work tackling them.

Answer the following questions to get yourself thinking. Then read through the rest of this chapter to find out where your problem areas are – and how to make them better. You'll be able to make positive changes, and see why having a boiler over fifteen years old, for example, is costing you money. Every inch of your home has money-saving potential – you just need to know what is being wasted, where, and how to fix it.

Ask yourself:

- What type of home do you have? (detached, flat, bungalow, etc.)
- How many floors does it have? (excluding the loft and cellar)
- Do you have a loft and is it insulated? (If 'yes', how thick is the insulation?)
- Do you have cavity-wall insulation?
- What sort of windows do you have?
- Do you have any draught-proofing?
- What sort of heating system does your home have?
- What sort of heating controls do you have?
- How old is your boiler?
- Do you have any hot-water controls?
- Is the hot-water tank insulated?
- Are the hot-water taps lagged?
- Do you have any low-energy light bulbs in your home? (If 'yes', how many?)
- In total, how many of the following appliances do you have? Fridge-freezer, fridge, freezer, washing machine, dishwasher, tumble dryer

Now you have this information, you can begin to ask yourself where you can make the biggest savings – in terms of energy and money.

Electric shock!

We spend £700 million every year on electricity to power a whole host of electric household gadgets — which means that we're demanding more and more energy from the power stations churning out all that pollution.

One of the best things we can do to offset the damage power stations cause to the environment is to switch to a 'green' energy supplier.

Green energy is energy generated by natural resources such as the sun, wind and water.

Some types of green energy:

● Wind power — from wind turbines, harnessed to generators that provide electricity
● Solar power — using solar panels to heat water, or generate electricity
● Wave power — Britain's coasts have some of the most powerful waves in the world
● Tidal power — powerful and predictable, the tides are 'always on'
● Geothermal power — from hot rocks deep in the Earth's crust, which cause water to boil and create steam that can drive turbines

Nearly all of the major utility companies provide a green tariff of some kind, so you may not even need to switch your current supplier.

You don't need any new cables or meters, as green electricity is delivered like normal electricity through the national grid. There's no extra effort by you — it's the supplier who makes sure that they buy a percentage of their electricity from renewable sources. This electricity is then fed back into the national grid, replacing traditional 'brown' electricity.

Look into the costs to see if it can work for you. There are two types of green tariff. With a renewable tariff, every unit of electricity bought by you is generated from renewable energy sources. Or, if you opt for an eco-funds tariff, which is an additional premium, this is invested in a fund and used to fund new renewable projects.

The more green electricity we purchase, the cleaner the supply coming through the national grid will be.

The Green Electricity Marketplace provides information on all the green tariffs available – check out www.greenelectricity.org.

Get switched on

We're a nation obsessed with interior design, and the average household lighting bill has rocketed. Long gone are the days when our living room was lit with a single bulb dangling from the centre of the ceiling. These days our living rooms are full of up-lighters, spotlights, halogens and wall lights. Overall Britain's domestic lighting bill is now about £1.2 billion a year.

In most homes, lighting accounts for around 10 to 15 per cent of the electricity bill, and it's easy to reduce the amount of energy you use to light your home.

We could reduce the amount of domestic energy we waste by 75 per cent simply by fitting long-lasting, highly efficient light bulbs.

They may cost a bit more than standard bulbs but they last far longer. According to the Energy Saving Trust, an energy-saving light bulb will cost you around £3.50 compared to 50p for a regular bulb, but it will save you around £9 on your annual electricity bill and up to £100 over its lifetime!

Energy-saving bulbs are particularly good in areas where lights need to be left on for a long time. They're great for outdoor security lights – you can even buy energy-efficient light bulbs with sensors that switch them on at dusk, and off again at dawn. Also, if children won't go to sleep unless there's a light left on in the hall, use an energy-saving one. Energy-saving lighting comes in all shapes and sizes now, and is much more effective than the original energy-saving bulbs, so you can be design conscious and less wasteful at the same time.

Switch off unnecessary lights.

The heat is on

Anything that generates heat is notoriously energy-hungry. And we want our homes to be warm and comfortable, so we need to ensure that we're using heating as efficiently as we possibly can.

- Use energy-efficient means of heat production (boilers etc.)
- Only heat rooms that you use, when you're using them

Some heating systems are more controllable than others, but the aim is the same: heat the rooms you want to, at the most suitable temperature, at the times of day you need to – and as cheaply as possible.

It's generally recommended that room temperatures should be somewhere between 18 and 21°C. Keeping the temperature at a reasonable level means that heat is lost more slowly to the outside air.

It's even better if you're able to adjust your heating appliances to give you what you need, when you need it. Room thermostats are usually placed on the living room wall or in the hallway and they respond to the temperature in that room. When the room has heated up enough the thermostat sends a signal to the central-heating pump to stop churning out heat, and that means water is no longer circulated around the radiators.

Some thermostats can be fitted to gas fires or electric heaters, or you can install thermostatic radiator values, which allow you to control the temperature in rooms other than the one in which the main thermostat for your heating system is placed.

As a general rule, you only need to heat occupied rooms. Although some heat is needed in other rooms to prevent condensation and damp building up, this heat can be kept fairly low.

If you want your heating to come on when you first get up to make your morning cuppa, and for the house to be nice and warm again before you get in from work, the best way to do it is by having an automatically controlled timer system installed. This controls the times at which the heating and hot-water systems come on and off. The simplest models have a time switch, whereas the most sophisticated allow different programming of heat and hot water for each day of the week.

Heat the rooms you want to, at the most suitable temperature, at the times of day you need to as cheaply as possible.

Getting into hot water

If your boiler is fifteen years old or more, and you replace it with a new, more energy-efficient version, you could save over 40 per cent on your fuel bills.

Condensing boilers are the most energy-efficient type of boiler on the market and could save you around a third on your bills straight away. And if you plump for a modern heating control system at the same time, then you could save even more. Visit www.boilers.org.uk to compare old and new boilers.

Uninsulated hot-water tanks lose a lot of heat, so insulating them should be a top priority, as an insulating jacket only costs a few pounds from a DIY store and pays for itself within a few months. If you go for one that's 75mm thick you could save up to £15 a year. Jackets come in a range of standard sizes and are fitted with belts that fasten snugly around the tank, so it's something you can easily do yourself.

The insulation reduces the heat loss from the tank, so less heat will be needed to keep the water at the correct temperature.

POTENTIAL SAVING

Insulating hot water tank
Cost = £5–10
Saving = £10–15 (per annum)

You should also insulate hot-water pipes to reduce heat loss. You can use lengths of rigid foam tubing, which you cut to size and then simply clip into place around the pipes. Again, this costs very little and can be done quite easily.

Radical radiators

Put foil behind your radiators that are against outside walls, and this will help to reflect heat back into your rooms. The extra warmth in the room may even mean you can turn down the thermostat a touch and make even more savings on your bills. Normal kitchen foil pasted to a board will do, or you can buy specially designed foil from a DIY store.

POTENTIAL SAVING

Foil behind radiators
Cost = up to £10
Saving = £10 – 15 (per annum)

Putting shelves up above your radiators is another good idea, helping you to save as much heat as possible by deflecting it back into the room. That can save you around five to ten pounds a year. The shelf should be fitted a couple of inches above the radiator for it to have maximum effect. It also helps if you move furniture away from radiators too, as furniture stops the heat from getting out and warming up the room effectively.

Insulation nation

By using efficient methods to heat our homes, and keeping that heat in – by insulation – we can do our bit to reduce the amount of energy we consume. And keep the fuel bills down at the same time!

Total heat loss in a typical house
Windows – up to 10%
Walls – up to 35%
Floor – up to 15%
Roof – up to 25%
Draughts – up to 15%

Windows and doors
You can tackle the heat lost from windows and doors in two ways:
● Don't leave doors and windows open needlessly
● Fit appropriate draught-proofing

Fitting draught brushes to the bottom of doors and adding seals to the doorframes will help to reduce draughts. You can also fit the letterbox with a cover and draughty keyholes can be covered too.

The amount of heat lost through windows depends on the type of frames you have and whether or not your windows have any kind of secondary glazing. Metal window frames, for instance, are really good at conducting heat from our homes to the cold outside world, which means that a lot of heat is lost through them. Wooden frames, on the other hand, are poor heat conductors, so heat tends to stays in the room for longer. Well-fitting windows are important, too. The older your house, the more likely you are to have windows that don't fit properly and cold air can blow in through the gaps. If this is the case, it may be cost efficient to have the windows replaced.

Double glazing is a fantastic way to conserve heat. The cheapest and simplest way to 'double-glaze' a window is to attach some form of plastic sheeting over it. Most DIY shops sell kits for a reasonable price and range from clingfilm-type materials to more long-lasting plastic sheeting.

The clingfilm version is the most inexpensive. It is available in a variety of large widths that can be cut to size depending on the shape and size of your windows. Basically, you attach double-sided tape to the inner face of the window frame and then use a hairdryer to stretch the clingfilm taut. It's a bit fiddly, but once you've done one you'll soon get the hang of it. However, it will only last for one winter season and you won't be able to open the windows you've sealed.

Another alternative is to buy flexible plastic sheeting. This is still fairly inexpensive, and has the advantage that you can take it down and reuse it each winter. As with any form of double glazing, it's important to check that there is adequate ventilation left in the room, and that you can still open at least one window.

Windows nearly always need some sort of covering – for privacy as well as to keep heat in, and curtains are the most obvious choice.

Curtain tips:

● Invest in curtains that are well fitted and preferably lined. You can buy thermal lining from most good fabric stores, and it only costs a few pounds a metre.

● Try to choose thick fabric that will keep the heat in and make sure you go for fullness, so when you close your curtains there are lots of folds in them – the gaps help to trap warm air.

● Draw your curtains at dusk and open them first thing in the morning. This enables you to make the most of 'passive solar gain', which means using the sun to heat your room, without costing a penny.

POTENTIAL SAVING
Draught-proofing windows and doors
Cost = £45–50
Saving = £10–20 (per annum)
Secondary glazing
Cost = £40–600
Saving = £15–25 (per annum)
Double glazing
Cost = £2,000+
Saving = £20–35 (per annum)

Walls
Most heat is lost through the walls of a house, but you can remedy this in a number of ways, and reduce heat loss by two-thirds.

Cavity walls
If you're lucky enough to have cavity walls, they can usually be filled with a special insulating material. The heat conserved by cavity-wall insulation can save you £70 to £100 a year. However, cavity-wall insulation must be carried out by professionals and the costs are quite high – although some grants may be available.

Solid walls
If you have solid walls, then you could go for some type of internal or external insulation – once again, this must be left to the professionals. Internal insulation involves some kind of insulated board fixed to the internal walls. However, it means that the rooms will need to be

redecorated. With external insulation, a heat-conserving finish is added to the house's exterior. This is more expensive and time-consuming to apply than internal insulation.

POTENTIAL SAVING

Cavity wall insulation
Cost = £300–400
Saving = £60–70 (per annum)
Internal wall insulation
Cost = £700–2,000
Saving = £40–60 (per annum)
External wall insulation
Cost = £2,000+
Saving = £55–85
Source: National Energy Foundation

The percentage levels above are dependent on several factors such as when your home was built. It's unlikely that your home will leak the maximum percentage on each area of loss, but there will be weak areas that you could address.

Floors

You can lose as much as 10 per cent of heat through uninsulated floors. Heat escapes as a result of gaps in floorboards, and even more near outside walls where heat escapes more quickly because the floor is in contact with colder earth at the sides of the house.

Once again, insulation is the key. Cover the floor with underlay, carpet, mats, woodblocks or cork tiles.

POTENTIAL SAVING
Depending on the materials, you could save £200 (per annum)

Roofs
A high proportion of the heat that escapes from our homes goes through our roofs. You can save as much as 25 per cent of your heating bill by making sure you've got good loft insulation.

Effective loft insulation needs to be at least 150mm deep, and preferably at least 200mm. Two materials can be used to insulate loft spaces – the most common is a roll of insulating material, which you can lay yourself. Alternatively, loose-filled materials can be poured between the joists to an even depth – this is a job for professionals.

Although self-laid loft insulation is generally seen to be one of the easiest DIY jobs, it's important to ensure you install it correctly to achieve the full potential. So, if you're going to tackle this yourself make sure you get the right tools for the job. You must wear protective clothing (goggles, a face mask and gloves), as insulation materials can be very irritating to the eyes, skin and throat. Any DIY store can provide you with this equipment as well as leaflets that explain how to do the job.

POTENTIAL SAVING
Cost = £150–300
Savings = £60–80 (per annum)

All about air

Draughts are a clear sign that your home's losing precious heat – which means that you're wasting energy, and the money you're spending on heating your home is wasted money. Draught-proofing will also improve the comfort level of your home. It's a job that most of you could tackle yourselves.

Draught-proofing strips are relatively cheap to buy and can be picked up from any good DIY store. However, make sure your house still has sufficient ventilation to prevent condensation and mildew.

> **Safety warning:** It's also vital for gas appliances to get a good supply of fresh air. They need this to burn efficiently and to take away harmful fumes. Whatever you do don't go blocking up air vents or grilles in the walls. There must be adequate ventilation in every room where there are any heating appliances such as boilers or open-flue gas-water heaters.

In 'wet' areas such as kitchens and bathrooms, think about installing heat-exchange units with a built-in humidistat. These cut your heat costs by reducing moisture and extracting warm air then returning it to the room. Contact Ventaxia (www.vent-axia.com) for more details.

ENERGY-EFFICIENT APPLIANCES
Cookers

Changing your cooking habits can do a lot to prevent waste – of food, energy, raw materials and money.

If you don't know how to cook – why not learn? Make your own ready-meals by doubling up on quantities and freezing one half for a later date. Other energy-saving tips:

- Don't fill the kettle to the top when you only want water for a cup of tea.
- When cooking, make sure you choose the right pan size for the food you're cooking – you don't want to heat a bigger pan than you need.
- Put lids on pans and food will cook much quicker, saving more energy.

Microwaves – good or bad?

Microwaves are a fairly energy-efficient method of cooking. However, much of the food we cook in microwaves is the pre-packaged ready-meal variety, which is neither good for the environment or our health.

Make use of the microwave's good points, by using them for defrosting food, or just warming things up.

Fridges and freezers

Fridges and freezers are real workhorses – unlike other appliances, you can't switch them off every day.

In Britain, we spend around £1.2 billion on electricity just to run our fridges and freezers each day. A high proportion of that electricity is wasted, because many of us are using old fridges and freezers that use more power than is necessary.

In fact, they may be costing us more in electricity bills than the price of a new one.

An energy-efficient fridge-freezer uses nearly a third of the energy to do the same job as a ten-year old appliance. That could amount to a saving of £45 a year on your fuel bill.

Other ways of cutting costs:

● Don't leave the fridge or freezer door open any longer than you need to – it takes three to four minutes for it to regain its correct temperature, which means you're wasting energy unnecessarily.

● Don't put hot food into the fridge – this raises the temperature inside, so you're just making it work harder than it needs to. You could also risk food poisoning if you cause the fridge temperature to rise higher than it should for too long.

● Defrost your freezer regularly.

● Check that the door seals are working properly. The seals should be tight enough to hold a piece of paper securely when the doors are closed.

● Keep your freezer packed full, but not your fridge. There should be plenty of room for air to circulate in the fridge.

Washing machines

Washing machines use loads of water, so try to put them on only when they're full. That way you make the most of the water and electricity they use. Most machines have half-load or 'eco-wash' buttons, and you should try to use those wherever possible.

It's also worth looking out for the energy label when buying a new washing machine or dishwasher, as they'll show you whether the appliance is water and energy efficient – the water consumption should be less than 55 litres per cycle. A washing machine uses on average 80 litres of water, which is five times more than a large sink full of water.

Washing tips:

● Only wash clothes when they're dirty. If you've only worn an item once and it's still spotless and doesn't smell, hang it outside or in the bathroom when you shower to freshen it up. This saves time, energy, water, and prolongs the life of the garment too.

● Go for a 40°C wash cycle rather than 60°C. You'll be using a third less electricity.

● Reduce the wash to a 30°C cycle and the amount of electricity and money saved will be even higher. Unless you have very dirty and heavily soiled clothes you really don't need a high-temperature wash.

Dishwashers

These are another water and energy guzzler, but an energy-efficient dishwasher will cut energy wastage by half. When using your dishwasher, like your washing machine, it's best to wait for a full load or use the economy cycle if your model has one.

Tumble dryers

If you really must buy a tumble dryer, make sure you buy the most energy-efficient model you can as it could cut energy wastage by almost a third. Avoid trying to dry really wet clothes – wring them out by hand or spin them dry first. Not only will the clothes dry faster, but you'll save energy and money.

POTENTIAL SAVING

By simply changing the way you use electronic products you could cut your energy bills by a quarter!

Look out for the logo

Look out for the Energy Label on fridges, freezers, washing machines, tumble dryers and dishwashers. They will explain what you're getting for your money in terms of how much the appliance costs to run, how well it performs, how much water it uses and even how noisy it is.

The more efficient the appliance, the less energy it needs to do the same job, so the more you get for your money, and the less damage you're doing to the environment.

The label also tells you how much electricity the appliance used in standard tests. You can use this information to work out how much you might save if you choose different types of models. Actual savings will, of course, depend on how you use the appliance and how much you pay for your electricity.

A-rated appliances are the most energy efficient with G-rated being the least efficient.

Washing wasters

On average, a person in a developed country such as the UK uses about 150 to 160 litres of water a day and we tend to use it in the home in the following ways:

Activity	Average amount of water used in litres
Taking a bath	120 litres
Running taps	1 litre
Washing	8 litres
Brushing our teeth	2 litres
Taking a shower	30 litres
Flushing the toilet	40 litres
Washing clothes in a washing machine	120 litres
Using a dishwasher	60 litres
Watering the garden using a sprinkler	60 litres
Washing the car with a hose pipe	90 litres

The Thames Water region uses 55 per cent of available rainfall. Another 800,000 people will be living in London by 2016 – the equivalent of the population of Leeds. We will need to find an extra 128 million litres of water per day to supply them.

We really do take water for granted. After all, we simply turn on a tap and out it comes. However, only 3 per cent of the water on our planet is fresh water – the other 97 per cent is undrinkable sea water. What's more, two thirds of that 3 per cent of fresh water is solid – it's locked up in the ice caps. This means that around only 1 per cent of the planet's water is available for us to drink.

Every time we use water it has to be cleaned. Most of the water we use ends up down a sewer, and is eventually transferred to a sewage treatment works. With increased flooding, sewers can overflow and this raw sewage can find its way back into rivers and other water supplies.

What you can do to save water:

● **DO** take a shower instead of a bath – a five-minute shower uses up about a third as much water as an average bath.

● **DO** make sure you turn taps off fully. A dripping tap can waste as much as ten litres a day.

● **DO** use a bowl of water to wash fruit and vegetables instead of running them under the tap.

● **DON'T** use more water than you need.

● **DON'T** leave the taps running when you're cleaning your teeth.

● **DON'T** allow the tap to run until the water is icy cold when you want a drink. Fill up a jug and keep it in the fridge instead.

● **DON'T** fill the bath right up when you run it. A full bath can hold more than 120 litres of water.

And to avoid contributing to water pollution:

● **DO** use environmentally friendly household cleaning products where you can. Or alternatively try using borax or vinegar to clean the bathroom.

● **DON'T** use too much detergent when washing up and hold back on pouring in the powder to your washing machine. Even environmentally friendly detergents need to be treated to some extent.

● **NEVER** pour oil, paint or any other chemical liquid down the drain or toilet.

● **TRY NOT** to use bleach or other disinfectant unless it's really unavoidable.

Fix that tap!

A dripping tap can waste a bathful of water every week, so make sure you fix any dripping taps in the home.

If you think there's a leak in your property (maybe you've had an unexpectedly high water bill) then report it to your water company. It's your responsibility to fix any leaks, but keep any plumber's receipts, as you may be able to claim a refund from your water supplier. If you're not sure who your water supplier is, www.water.org.uk will tell you.

Money down the pan

Toilets are huge water guzzlers, accounting for 35 per cent of domestic water use. We can easily flush away 100 litres of water per person per day. Old toilets use 9.5 litres each flush, although those installed since 1993 use only 7.5 litres. We don't need to use so much water when flushing, so here are some ideas to cut down.

Put a water 'hippo' bag, a full plastic bottle, or anything that will take up space, into the cistern. 'Hippos' will save up to three litres of water with every flush. If one toilet is flushed ten times a day, this equates to a water saving of about 25 litres per day – that's enough for a five-minute shower.

Does your toilet have an eco-flush? If so, make use of it! This clever little invention offers the user a choice of flush with high and low settings. This could reduce water used to flush the toilet by a third. It takes a few days to get into the habit of selecting the right setting, but it's well worth it for both the financial savings (if your water is metered) and the environment. Installation is fairly simple too.

Don't use the toilet as a dustbin. When sanitary products and condoms reach the sewage treatment plant, any blockages that occur mean that the sewage will eventually end up in rivers and the sea. Make sure that items like tampons, sanitary towels, disposable nappies, cotton buds, condoms and cigarettes are put in the bin instead of down the toilet.

Sexy suds

For those who want something a little more adventurous and amorous, how about sharing a bath to save water? Put on your favourite Barry White album – OK, that may not be to everyone's liking – light some scented candles, pour a glass of wine and sit back and relax together. It's a great way to wind down, spend some intimate time with your partner and de-stress after a hard day at work.

Speedy showers

This is so simple. Switch it on; get wet; switch off; soap up and wash; switch back on and rinse. Although baths are generally said to be more water-wasteful than showers, a power shower running for twenty minutes uses more water than having a bath. Being efficient in the way you shower will save money from going down the drain.

If you just do one thing ...

Try the five-minute shower challenge!

A 90-litre bath costs 25p whereas a five-minute shower uses only 25 litres of water, costing just 7p on a standard combi boiler.

Where to go for help
Energy Efficiency Advice Centres

Energy Efficiency Advice Centres provide free, expert and impartial advice on how to save energy and money. They can provide you with a free DIY Home Energy Check, which allows them to assess what the most cost-effective ways would be for you to save energy in your home.

They'll also tell you what grants are available in your area and provide details of your nearest approved professional installers, if you need one. In addition they can provide general information and tips on energy efficiency over the telephone, face to face, or through their leaflets and information packs.

Call the EEAC freephone hotline – 0800 512012 – during office hours. For a full list of UK EEACs refer to the Energy Saving Trust website (www.est.org.uk).

It's payback time

Some methods of energy saving are fairly cheap and simple enough for you to do yourself. Almost anyone could draught-proof their windows and doors or fit a jacket on the hot-water tank. Other jobs, however, such as double glazing and cavity-wall insulation, cost a great deal more and you will need professional installers. But they still help the planet, and save you money in the long run.

When you're thinking about being more energy efficient in your home you need to consider the payback period – this is the amount of time it will take for you to recoup the initial outlay. Although double glazing and cavity-wall insulation will significantly cut heat loss, it could still take a long time for the costs of what you've paid out to be regained through cheaper fuel bills.

No-cost tips

Stop using standby buttons – don't leave your TVs, videos, PCs and printers 'on' for the sake of convenience. If we all switched off our TVs at the socket, we could save enough energy to power a small town.

Switch it off – why not switch off your telly and talk or play a game instead?

Turn it down – if you turn your heating thermostat down by 1°C you will hardly notice the difference and it will cut your bills by 10 per cent a year. What's wrong with wearing jumpers in the winter? Be sensible, though. Don't turn the heating down below 20°C, especially if there are old or vulnerable people in the house, and don't shock your body by going from summer temperatures in your house to cold air outside.

Move it! – Move furniture away from radiators, to allow the warm air to circulate.

Don't boil too much – choose the right-sized pan for the food and cooker, put lids on pans, and don't overfill the kettle.

Keep that chill – defrost your freezer regularly and keep it packed full to avoid wasting energy. Check the seals are still intact to ensure no warm air is getting in.

Fill her up – try to use full loads when using your washing machine and use the low temperature wash of 40°C. On some washing machines, only cold water is used to fill the machine when it is set to a low temperature, which means that there is no need to heat up the central-heating boiler.

Soak up the rays – the sun is the most readily available source of heat we have – and the cheapest! Make the most of it by opening internal doors of any rooms that get more sun than others and let the warm air travel though your home on a summer's day. You can also make the most of available daylight, cutting your reliance on electric lighting.

Dry naturally – avoid using tumble dryers and radiators to dry your clothes – on a nice sunny or breezy day hang them outside instead and let them dry.

Don't be a drip – fix any leaky taps, as even a small drip can use a lot of water over time.

Low-cost tips

Better bulbs – fit energy-saving light bulbs; they use about a quarter of the electricity that normal 60-watt bulbs use. That could save you around seven to ten quid a year – and you won't have to change the blighters for years either, as they last for ages. Just seven low-energy bulbs could literally last you a lifetime – a good-quality low-energy bulb can last up to twelve years.

Block that draught – gaps in door and window frames are responsible for a fifth of wasted heat in our homes.

Insulate water tanks and pipes – fitting an insulating jacket to the hot-water tank will keep water hot and save up to £20 a year. Lagging pipes could save you an extra £5.

Insulate the loft – 250mm of loft insulation will shave a lot off your heating bills.

Look for the logo – buy energy-efficient appliances.

Seeing double – double-glazed windows reduce noise and condensation and keep the heat in, saving energy and reducing your fuel bills.

Install an energy-efficient boiler – a high-efficiency boiler could save up to 40 per cent on your fuel bills. Power companies and local authorities often provide grants to help meet the extra cost of installation.

Turn it down – lower the setting on your heating thermostat to 18 to 21°C. If you get chilly, wear a jumper.

Shock statistics

- Britain's energy wasting habits are the worst in Europe, and could waste £11 billion per year by 2010 (source: Energy Saving Trust).
- If every UK household installed just three energy-saving light bulbs we would save enough energy each year to run all of the country's street lighting.

USEFUL CONTACTS

Energy Saving Trust (www.est.org.uk) for loads of useful information on helping you to make the most of your energy.

National Energy Foundation (www.nef.org.uk) mobilises individuals, businesses and communities to make their contribution to reducing carbon emissions through energy efficiency and the use of sustainable energy sources in order to maintain the affordability of energy and to combat global warming.

3
Green driving

Air pollution from motor vehicles has become a major problem – both for the planet's health and our own – and the situation is set to worsen, as more and more vehicles clog up our roads.

Isn't it strange how much we're prepared to put up with, simply because we won't give up our cars? Smelly fumes, noise, traffic jams, endless rounds of diversions and road works, children screaming in the back seats and increased blood pressure – these have all become part of our everyday routines.

Cars are a definite eco-evil. But it's simply not practical for everyone to don a pair of sandals and set off on a twenty-mile route march to work every day. It *is* feasible, however, for everyone to use their cars (and motorbikes) a bit differently and to switch to alternative forms of transport wherever possible.

Causes of air pollution

Most vehicles use petrol or diesel made from oil, and their exhaust gases go straight into the air that we breathe.

Of course, we can't blame all air pollution from increased traffic use on people like us jumping into our cars at every opportunity we get. Not every vehicle on the roads is a family car. But if you join the dots and look at your lifestyle, you'll see that what you buy, how you shop, and what you throw away all has a direct link to increased traffic on the roads.

We're becoming more and more reliant on road transport for moving all the goods we buy – and if we're causing more pollution because of the goods we're demanding, then it's up to us to cut our consumption. It's the 'Reduce' part of the 3 Rs.

Traffic Statistics

- Across the UK, car availability is lowest in London, with 63 per cent of households owning a car. It's highest in the Southeast, where 80 per cent of households have at least one car and 33 per cent of households own two or more. (Source: National Travel Survey)

- In the UK, 84 per cent of people hear traffic noise at home: 40 per cent of people are bothered, annoyed or disturbed by it; and 28 per cent of people say that road-traffic noise at their homes has got worse over the past five years. (Source: Defra)

- A double-decker bus carries the same number of people as 20 fully laden cars. (Source: TravelWise)

- Women used taxis more than men in Britain in 1999/2001, with 13 per cent of women and 11 per cent of men using a taxi at least once a week. (Source: National Travel Survey)

- Men in Britain are keener cyclists than women, according to statistics from 1999/2001. They made 23 journeys per person per year overall compared with 9 journeys for women. (Source: National Travel Survey)

Greener cars – what you can do

Do you really need that second car? Why not buy a motor scooter, moped or small motorcycle instead? These are cheaper to buy and run, reduce traffic congestion and produce fewer emissions than cars. Even better, treat yourself to a bicycle.

Because of the raw materials and energy involved in making new cars, it makes green sense to buy second-hand – in effect you're 'recycling' someone else's perfectly good car. However, in favour of new cars is the fact that you might be able to buy one that's more fuel efficient and eco-friendly – the technology is advancing all the time.

When you need a new car, do your research and make a smarter, more informed choice – opt for a car with a smaller, less polluting engine. The more fuel that is burned, the more greenhouse gases are produced.

If you're buying a new car, go for the smallest and most economical possible. The Environmental Transport Association (ETA) online Car Buyer's Guide is a quick and easy way to see the environmental rating of all new cars on the market. Visit their website (www.eta.co.uk) for loads of green motoring tips.

Many cars can be converted to run on liquefied petroleum gas (LPG), or can be made to run on dual fuel (a mixture of LPG and petrol). However, LPG isn't cheap when compared to petrol, so a more economic alternative could be to convert a car to run as a hybrid.

Hybrids

A hybrid car has a petrol engine and an electric motor. When the car is braking, decelerating or cruising, the electric motor's batteries are charged, and this means you don't need to recharge the battery at a power point. There are already a few hybrid cars on the market in the UK and the biggest advantage is that their fuel consumption is as much as 30 per cent lower than equivalent petrol cars.

Electric cars

Wholly electric cars produce no emissions on the road, have lower fuel costs than their petrol equivalents, and maintenance is cheaper, too, because they have less moving parts to service and replace.

To refuel your electric car you simply need to plug it into the domestic mains supply for around seven hours. However, even though they don't belch out traffic fumes while they're being driven, the electricity used to power them has to be generated by a power station. So, unless you're on a green electricity tariff (see page 55), they still contribute to polluting emissions.

Some city centres now provide free parking and recharging ports for people using electric cars. The beauty of electric cars is that they can be recharged from virtually any standard 13-amp socket anywhere, and you can take advantage of off-peak rates to keep costs down.

Which car to choose?

Different types of fuel and vehicles have different environmental benefits and drawbacks. As the less familiar technology is still in its infancy, there are a few practical disadvantages – just as with any new technology before everyone begins using it.

For this reason, many people are more comfortable sticking to petrol or diesel cars. If you don't feel ready to take the plunge and go hybrid or electric in your driving, you can still be more environmentally friendly by choosing a car that produces a lower level of emissions and being aware of how you use your car.

Make sure you get your car serviced regularly at a garage – usually every 12 months or every 10,000 miles. A well-maintained car can use less fuel, so keep an eye on how much fuel you're using, as this can be a good indication that your car isn't working as efficiently as it could. Under-inflated tyres, for example, can increase fuel consumption by up to 8 per cent.

The health implications of traffic

Traffic is bad for our health. Just take a look at some of the pollutants that make up traffic fumes.

Carbon monoxide – reduces the amount of oxygen carried in the blood. High doses can cause headaches and vomiting.

Diesel smoke – can cause cancer.

Nitrogen oxides – irritate the throat and eyes.

Sulphur dioxide – causes coughing and a feeling of tightness in the chest.

Benzene – can cause a form of anaemia and is linked to leukaemia.

It makes for depressing reading, doesn't it? And the situation is getting worse. According to the National Travel Survey, walking – the most healthy form of travel – has decreased by 20 per cent in Britain since the mid-1980s, whereas car usage has shot up by 40 per cent in the same time period.

Shock statistics

- The health impacts of traffic pollution cost £11.1billion each year. (Source: Environmental Transport Association)
- A worrying 60 per cent of men and 70 per cent of women are so physically inactive that they risk coronary heart disease, diabetes, stroke or obesity. (Source: Health Education Authority)
- Children living on streets with heavy traffic are more likely to develop chronic respiratory problems. (Source: Occupational and Environmental Medicine)

'Greening' your travel habits
Your travel choices

Use your common sense (and sometimes your legs) instead of automatically using your car for every trip. Before making any journey you should ask yourself if it's really necessary to use the car. The shortest journeys (those less than two miles) are the biggest polluters because it often means our engines are cold and are straining to warm up – which means they use more fuel and create more pollution.

Look at the way you travel to work, and to social activities, and set yourself a weekly target for using the bus, train, walking or cycling, instead of using your car. Start off gently, and try to increase the amount of public transport, cycling and walking you use each month to ease yourself in gently. If you stick to your targets you'll soon feel the benefits of your greener, healthier lifestyle.

If it's too far to cycle or walk to the supermarket, why not use public transport to get there and back? Many of the larger supermarkets have bus stops in their grounds, so you don't have to struggle down the road to catch the bus, you can just hop straight on and off with your shopping.

Plan your journeys by checking public-transport websites (e.g. www. traveline.org.uk) and by ringing local public-transport providers for time-table information and fares. Ring local licensed taxi firms to get quotes and display 'car share' notices at work or, if you have children, at the school. Or you could check out www.liftshare.com or www.nationalcar-share.co.uk.

Plan combined trips, such as doing shopping during your work lunch hour, or cycling for exercise and calling in on your local shop for 'top-up' items, like bread and milk.

If you must use your car, make it worthwhile. If you really can't pull yourself away from using your car, could you share the journey with a friend or colleague?

If you have children, get their little legs working! Encourage them to walk or get them to cycle where it is safe to do so. A rota of parents could take it in turns to walk the kids to school. Or if cycling appeals, then visit Cycle Training UK's website www.cycletraining.co.uk – they are the UK's biggest independent provider of on-road cycle training, and they also provide cycle maintenance training in London. They train instructors throughout the UK, so are a good place to start to look for local instructors. Cycle Training UK also supplies tailor-made training for individuals and families.

Get on your bike!
It's good for your health and bikes are cheap to buy and maintain. What's more, they're free to use and park.

The way you drive
Apart from being dangerous, aggressive driving causes more pollution, and also means higher fuel costs. Try to avoid rapid acceleration and heavy braking – it will reduce your fuel use. Smoother and steadier driving can use 30 per cent less fuel. And obey the speed limit – if you don't, you're not only wasting fuel but you face a hefty fine or even a prison sentence.

Wearing the right footwear (flat and comfortable) helps you to control the accelerator and brake, as you'll be more sensitive to the pressure you need to apply. Abrupt braking and accelerating increases harmful emissions. So think about what you've got on your feet and consider buying some driving shoes if you haven't got anything suitable in your wardrobe.

> Driving at 50mph can use 25 per cent less fuel than at 70mph.

Remove any roof racks from your car if you're not using them, as they increase the wind resistance and that means you'll be using more fuel. Keeping unnecessary bulky items in the boot also adds to the weight of your car and increases fuel consumption.

Don't sit in your car with the engine idling. You're pumping out loads of pollution and it wastes fuel too. If you have a catalytic converter – which is a device that removes pollution in the exhaust – then sitting in your car with the engine running stops the catalytic converter from working properly.

> **If you do just one thing ...**
> Don't use the car for journeys that are only walking distance.

WHAT YOU CAN SAVE
- Up to £2,900 – this is what the average household spends on motoring in a year.

USEFUL CONTACTS

Traveline (www.traveline.org.uk) provides national public transport time-tables and information.

There are many car share schemes (e.g. www.liftshare.com or www.nationalcarshare.co.uk).

Cycle Training UK (www.cycletraining.co.uk) has loads of information on cycling and learning to ride a bike.

ETA (www.eta.co.uk) is a green, carbon-neutral, motoring information resouce.

4
Recycling

Sorting our household rubbish so that the maximum amount can be recycled is the 'green' thing to do. But how do we know what to recycle and how to recycle it?

And we know that buying 'greener' products that can be reused or recycled will help to reduce the drain we cause to the environment – but sometimes buying 'green' products can be confusing. What do all those symbols mean? And how can you tell if one product contains more recycled material than another?

What happens to waste?

What happens to our rubbish once it's collected by the binmen? It generally joins waste collected from parks, schools, factories, businesses and shopping centres. All this waste is known collectively as 'municipal waste'.

Usually, municipal waste gets sent to landfill sites, which are essentially enormous holes in the ground that our rubbish gets tipped into and buried – that is until it's impossible to squeeze any more in.

There are now thousands of managed landfill sites in the UK, but space for landfill is running out – and that's not the only problem. Landfill sites are smelly and can attract vermin such as rats, which spread disease. And despite the fact that the rubbish is buried underground, it produces large amounts of potentially toxic gases that escape to be released into the atmosphere.

Also, some bits of rubbish can be carried off in the wind and end up in the surrounding countryside. If all this isn't bad enough, liquid can seep into the soil from older sites – and this liquid can contain harmful chemicals such as pesticides, solvents and heavy metals, which contaminate our water supplies.

Some waste from sewage sludge is also buried in landfill sites, along with waste from mining and quarrying.

Dust from landfill sites has also been known to cause skin and eye irritation to those living nearby.

Landfill statistics

● Many areas of this country now have less than ten years of landfill space left and the quantity of rubbish we produce is rising by at least 3 per cent a year.

● If every home recycled 50 per cent of its rubbish the UK's annual carbon dioxode emissions would fall by six million tonnes.

A burning issue

Some waste is burned in specially built incinerators; of the 7,000 incinerators in England and Wales, just 12 burn municipal waste. However, the ashes that are left over from this process are then buried in a landfill site!

Incinerators also produce smoke, gas and fumes that contain potentially harmful chemicals, although the jury is still out on the damage these chemicals do to our health, and what they will do to the environment in the future.

Toxic tips

Some waste contains toxins that are harmful to human health even in very small quantities. And because many toxins don't break down once they're buried or released into the environment, there's always the danger that they will get passed back to us through the food we buy, the air we breathe and the water we drink.

You've got mail

Up to 20 per cent of the mail that comes through your letterbox is never opened, and up to 60 per cent is never read. Here's somewhere where we can bring in the first of the 3 Rs – Reduce. If we can stop 'junk mail' coming through our letterboxes in the first place then we can avoid all the waste and pollution it takes to produce and distribute it – and then to dispose of it.

Sign up to the Mailing Preference Service (www.mpsonline.org.uk) to remove your name from all direct-mailing lists. However, the MPS cannot remove your name from the mailing lists of companies you have actually purchased from or charities you have donated to. To stop receiving this kind of mail you will have to contact the relevant organisations directly.

RECYCLING – The practicalities

Most people think recycling is the hardest part of any lifestyle change, but it's actually simple – you just need to open your eyes and roll your sleeves up a bit.

All of us have a major part to play in helping to reduce our rubbish and increase recycling and composting. It is essential for safeguarding the planet, as well as our long-term health and wellbeing.

The less rubbish we send to landfill sites or to incinerators, the more valuable materials and energy we save. Sorting out the materials in our household waste ready for recycling helps in many ways. Unlike burying and burning rubbish, recycling allows materials to be used again and made into other useful products. For example, plastic can be recycled to make office furniture, sleeping bags can be produced using shredded telephone directories and that fleece you're wearing could well be made from a batch of recycled plastic drinks bottles!

Paper and cardboard

Recycling paper uses 30 to 70 per cent less energy than producing paper from virgin materials, and reduces the pressure on natural resources. There should be a paper-bank recycling facility near you – but make sure you put only the correct type of paper in the recycling bank. Some, for instance, don't want the glossy 'coated' papers that are used in magazines and on some types of packaging.

Recycled products can contain varying amounts of recycled materials. Recycled papers, for example, can be produced using different amounts of recycled waste, and be made from different grades of waste paper. A paper product isn't considered to be recycled unless it contains at least 51 per cent post-consumer waste, so products with 100 per cent post-consumer waste content are the most environmentally friendly. Recycled paper can be used for all sorts of things including toilet roll, cat litter, kitchen towels, stationery and animal bedding.

Metals

Waste metal makes up around 8 per cent of the contents of the average household dustbin contents – but recycling it is simple. Just wash your tins and cans, and put them in the appropriate bin for collection and recycling.

Plastics

Visit www.recoup.org for more details on different types of plastic and where you can recycle them. We still have a long way to go where recycling plastic in the UK is concerned; but gradually more and more companies are realising that there is profit in plastic waste.

Electronic equipment

Since the beginning of 2007 the WEEE (Waste Electrical and Electronic Equipment) Directive will mean that no electronic equipment can be disposed of in landfill, which will reduce pollution and cut the volume of waste going to landfill. However, many local authorities provide a free service for households to get rid of electrical items, so give them a call first to see what's on offer. Try Action Aid's National Recycling Scheme for ink and toner cartridges, mobile phones and PDAs to raise funds for the charity (www.actionaidrecycling.org.uk).

If you've really finished with that computer, send it to be refurbished or resold. Many international charities or schools can benefit from your unwanted equipment. Try Computer Aid International (www. computeraid.org).

Batteries

Many older types of battery contain potentially harmful metals such as mercury and cadmium, and there are so many different sizes and types of batteries that sorting and recycling can be difficult. Rechargeable nickel cadmium batteries can be recycled – visit www.rebat.com for more details. Other types of battery are more tricky, so try not to use them. Use rechargeable batteries, or power items from the mains instead.

> Why not invest in a solar powered or wind-up radio or torch? Wind-up versions are great in a power cut!

The big stuff

Recycling really large items requires a bit more effort, but you'll be making a huge difference in helping to reduce your waste. Recycling can go much further than the contents of your dustbin.

If you're replacing your fridge, freezer, washing machine or any other appliance with a nice new energy-efficient one, ask your local council if they can collect your old one and recycle or dispose of it properly.

When it comes to furnishings, you can still be environmentally responsible without your home screaming 'eco-freak!' Good-quality second-hand furniture can be great. It's not so difficult to retrieve and revitalise beautiful pieces like carved wardrobes, chests of drawers, tables, chairs and cabinets.

If you really don't want a piece of furniture any more and it's still in good condition, you should see if you can get it collected – someone else might love it.

You can also donate furniture in good condition to a charity or your local sports club for use in the clubhouse – some may collect it for free. Also, the Furniture Re-use Network (www.frn.org.uk) co-ordinates over 300 projects in the UK.

If you've got loads of stuff to clear out, then why not take it to a car-boot sale and make yourself some pocket money? There are also loads of local charities who can find a good home for all kinds of clothes and household items you may no longer need or want.

Garden and kitchen waste

Instead of binning it, try composting your garden and veggie peelings. It's an easy process and not only will your dustbin be less full and less smelly, you'll also be improving your local environment and even saving money in the bargain. If you don't have a garden to compost in, some areas have set up community composting sites. Visit the Community Composting Network (www.communitycompost.org) for more information.

You'll also find more on composting on page 161.

Glass

Glass is one of the best materials for recycling, as it can be recycled again and again, saving energy and raw materials each time. Before recycling your glass, make sure the bottles and jars are washed, and any tops or plastic attachments removed. Do try and put your glass in the right-coloured banks – any contamination will lower the value of the recycled glass.

Many companies and craftspeople produce glassware from recycled glass. Just type 'recycled glassware' or something similar into an Internet search engine and see what you find.

Recycling – where to take it
97

Recycling

Bank schemes

Most local authorities now provide local recycling collection points for glass, newspapers and magazines. Some also provide banks for plastics, textiles, books or aluminium foil.

Visit www.recycle-more.co.uk to find out where the recycling banks are in your area.

Kerbside collections

In addition, many local authorities operate door-to-door (or 'kerbside') collection schemes for some items such as tin cans. Schemes for domestic composting are also growing in popularity. Contact your local authority for further information.

Civic Amenity Sites

Civic Amenity Sites were initially provided as a separate facility from land-fill sites, to allow the public free disposal of bulky domestic waste. These sites are now operated on behalf of county or unitary district waste disposal authorities, and are often called Household Waste Recycling Centres. For details of your nearest Civic Amenity Site and details of all the recycling services in your area contact your local council's recycling officer.

For all household waste and recycling information and enquiries visit the Waste Watch website (www.wastewatch.org.uk).

Shock statistics

● Recycling aluminium uses only 5 per cent of the energy needed

>>

>>

to make it from bauxite (aluminium ore). That's a 95 per cent energy saving. (Source: Alupro.org.uk)

● Over 1.5 million computers are dumped in landfill sites every year in the UK.

● Around 7 per cent of the contents of your dustbin is likely to be plastic.

Get yourself a new recycling toy – the Crush-a-Can

Show your support for the environment by using your feet – you can squash cans to make them take up less space in your recycling bin. Or you could buy a Crush-a-Can from Lakeland (www.lakeland limited.com) that easily flattens bulky aluminium and steel cans safely, ready for recycling. The Crush-a-Can takes cans up to 475ml and costs around £12.95.

Buying recycled

By buying recycled products, you're doing your bit for the environment by reducing the raw materials that are used to make 'new' products. Recycled products are generally easier to recycle again as well.

Jargon Buster

Get to know your recycling terms.

Recyclable – this is pretty self-explanatory! Many products made from glass, metal, paper or plastic can be recycled and you can take them to your local authority's recycling centres. Just make sure you put the right materials in the right bins (e.g. no green bottles in the brown bottle bank). Many of the large supermarkets or main shopping centres provide recycling banks so you could use those facilities when you're getting your weekly shopping.

Recycled content – some products are labelled as 'recycled' even when the amount of recycled content is quite low. And sometimes it's not clear if this claim applies to the product/content or the packaging. Companies are supposed to make their claims clear and nonambiguous (see the Green Claims Code, page 30), but unfortunately some claims can still cause confusion. A non-misleading and clear claim will tell you what percentage of the product/content (and/or packaging) is recycled or recyclable.

Biodegradable – this means that a product will break down naturally in the soil or in water. However, the length of time this takes depends on the material. Some products and packaging take many years to break down and will release harmful substances or gases in the process. Again, check that the claim really explains what is meant by biodegradable, as most everyday products biodegrade eventually – but if that means in 200 years time, then it's not really helpful!

Learning the logos

It's not always easy to find out if one product really is more 'green' than another. A lot of products carry environmental claims and labels, and whilst some of these give useful information on what the product is made from, or the best way to use it or dispose of it, others are so vague they have little real value to us as purchasers.

Here's a run-down of the main 'green' symbols and logos:

Möbius loop

The Möbius loop is probably the most familiar symbol associated with recycling. Essentially, it shows that something is capable of being recycled. However, as a product with a Möbius loop logo wasn't necessarily made from recycled material itself, it can be misleading if more information isn't provided on the product label.

In the example shown, the use of the Möbius loop is more meaningful, because it shows that a particular product or object contains a percentage of recycled material. However, the use of this symbol is voluntary.

Energy efficiency

Most energy-efficient appliances cost no more than any other, and will certainly save money and energy over their lifetime.

The EU energy label

Manufacturers and retailers must, by law, tell you about the energy efficiency of a range of electrical appliances such as washing machines,

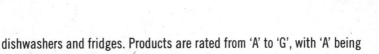

dishwashers and fridges. Products are rated from 'A' to 'G', with 'A' being the most efficient and 'G' the least efficient.

Energy Efficiency logo

Energy Efficiency is a government-backed initiative run by the Energy Saving Trust and is aimed at raising awareness of the benefits of energy-efficient products that save you money and energy, and help to protect the environment. The Energy Saving Trust's blue and orange Energy Efficiency logo appears on a range of products – from light bulbs to boilers and laundry appliances – and indicates the most energy-efficient appliances on the market.

The European Union Ecolabel

The European Union 'flower' Ecolabel can be found on a wide range of household goods, including electrical appliances, kitchen towels, toilet rolls, textiles, washing powder, paint and compost. The manufacturers have to meet high environmental standards in order to use this symbol on their products. For example, appliances must be energy efficient, and manufacturing processes must have minimal impact on the environment.

Glass

This symbol shows that glass can be recycled – but make sure that when you take your bottles to the bottle banks you put the right-coloured glass in the right banks. It's too easy to mix up green and brown bottles, but the cost of sorting out these mistakes can be huge.

Metals

Both aluminium and steel cans can be recycled. Look for these logos on your food, drink and aerosol cans. When recycling food and drink cans, rinse them out first so they are clean.

Recyclable aluminium

Recyclable steel

recyclable steel

Paper

National Association of Paper Merchants

To be given this mark, paper or board must be made from a minimum of 75 per cent genuine waste paper or board fibre, no part of which should contain mill-produced waste fibre.

Wood

The Forestry Stewardship Council (FSC) logo identifies products that contain wood from well-managed forests, which are independently certified in accordance with the FSC's rules.

Low VOC content

VOCs are volatile organic compounds, which can be harmful to human health, causing headaches and dizziness, and exacerbating breathing problems such as asthma. It's possible that long-term exposure to VOCs could increase our risk of certain cancers. VOCs are found in many paints and household cleaning agents. Look for labels that show a minimum or low VOC content, and use water-based paints where possible. Contact the

Association for Conscious Building on 0845 4569773 (www.aecb.net) for information on nontoxic paints.

Plastics

There are various types of plastic. Different plastics have to be recycled in different ways – check the specific details of the recycling scheme you use. You may not be able to recycle all of the kinds of plastics in your bin, so you need to know what kind of plastic is in each product or container. The different types are:

Polyethylene terephthalate (PET or PETP)

This logo is found on the bottom of many plastic bottles, containers for food products and carbonated soft drinks.

High density polyethylene (HDPE)

Found in containers for milk, household cleaning products and containers for cosmetics, shampoos and deodorants.

Polyvinyl chloride (PVC)

Found in a wide range of consumer products such as clingfilm, bottles, credit cards, audio records and imitation leather, as well as materials such as window frames, cables, pipes and flooring. It is also used in car interiors and by hospitals for medical disposables. The production of PVC creates and releases one of the most toxic chemicals, dioxin.

Polypropylene

Found in clothes, bottles, containers, caps and moisture-proof wrapping.

Polycarbonate
Found in plastic baby bottles, beakers and tableware.

Chlorofluorocarbons (CFCs)
These are used to produce expanded polystyrene, but alternatives are being sought.

Polystyrene
Found in kitchen utensils or, in an expanded form, in insulation and ceiling tiles. It is produced in three main forms:
● Foamed polystyrene (PS-E): This is used in clamshell containers (e.g. those used for fast food), meat trays and egg cartons. It is also used in loose-fill and moulded protective packaging for shipping electronic goods and other fragile items.
● High-impact polystyrene (PS-HI): This is used in thermo-formed containers for dairy products.
● Crystal polystyrene (GPPS): This is a clear and brittle material used to make CD jewel cases, bottles for pills, tablets, capsules and thin-walled cups.

TOP FIVE TIPS
1. Sort your rubbish into things that can and cannot be recycled
2. Find the location of your nearest recycling point
3. Learn the logos – for recycled and recyclable products
4. Buy recycled and recyclable products where possible
5. Reduce your reliance on materials that are hard to recycle, such as certain plastics

USEFUL CONTACTS
Reducing waste
The Mailing Preference Service (www.mpsonline.org.uk) can remove your name from the mailing lists of companies you don't want to hear from.

General recycling information
The Department for Environment, Food and Rural Affairs (Defra) website (www.defra.gov.uk) includes a copy of the Green Claims Code and more information on the European Union Ecolabel and EU energy label.

Green Choices (www.greenchoices.org) provides a mass of information for those wishing to make green choices, including details of many recycled products for the home.

Waste Online (www.wasteonline.org.uk) provides a wealth of recycling and other green information.

Recycle More (www.recycle-more.co.uk) has loads of information on all aspects of recycling, with plenty of practical advice.

Waste Watch (www.wastewatch.org.uk) provides information about what and where you can recycle. It also produces useful fact sheets on materials such as plastics and batteries that can be tricky to find recycling facilities for.

How to recycle
WRAP (www.wrap.org.uk) works directly with the public sector, with community groups and with schools, to help people reduce their waste and recycle more stuff, more often.

Recycle Now (www.recyclenow.co.uk) will tell you where to find your nearest recycling bank, and give information on how to make a difference by recycling.

Recycle More (www.recycle-more.co.uk) shows you how to increase recycling rates in your home and provides more information on recycling labels and what they mean.

Waste Connect (www.wasteconnect.co.uk) is a handy database that lists every recycling facility in the country. Simply type in your postcode to find what's available in your area.

Alupro (www.Alupro.org.uk) has plenty of information on recycling aluminium.

Recoup (www.recoup.org) has information on recycling plastics.

Action Aid (www.actionaidrecycling.org.uk) will recycle your ink and toner cartridges, mobile phones and PDAs.

Computer Aid (www.computeraid.org) disposes of your PC ethically by sending it to a developing country.

Furniture Re-use Network (www.frn.org.uk) can find a new home for your old furniture.

Recycled and recycling products

The UK's directory of recycled products can be found at www.recycledproducts.org.uk.

Waste Watch's UK recycled products guide tells you where you can buy recycled goods of all kinds. Look up www.recycledproducts.org.uk or telephone 0870 243 0136

The Natural Collection catalogue (www.naturalcollection.com or tel: 0870 331 3333) has a wide range of environmentally friendly and recycled products. Friends of the Earth receive a donation from sales.

Lakeland Limited's wide range of products includes many with a 'green' slant, including a can crusher, recycling bins and bags (including a bin with separate compartments), carrier bag stores, a composting crock, and several products made from recycled materials.

For information on environmentally friendly building, contact the **Association for Environment Conscious Building** on 0845 4569773 (www.aecb.net).

5
De-clutter
your life

Being wasteful in the home isn't just about plastic packaging and leaving the lights on all day; it's also about how we waste time, how we expend physical and mental energy, and how we use and protect our personal space.

We're all leading increasingly busy lives and that means spending less time doing the things we want to do – and having less time for the ones we love.

As a first step, if you banish clutter, you'll feel more relaxed, less stressed and you'll regain control of your life.

Time and space

We need to guard our time carefully, otherwise our personal 'free time' can suddenly vanish because we have to go and visit the in-laws, or take those forms we meant to post to the local tax office. The secret is to plan ahead and make sure everyone knows what you're planning – otherwise you'll find there's an ever-increasing list of demands being made on your time and you end up having no time to do the things you want to do.

Be selfish with your time

Make sure that you earmark a regular few hours on the calendar as 'family time'. That way, you're much more likely to stick to it. It doesn't matter if you haven't made any definite plans like going to play football in the park with the kids, or going for a country walk. If it rains, you can rent a film instead or play a board game for a couple of hours. The point is, you've allocated that time for you and for them and you're sticking to it.

Me time

Above all, being organised and taking control of your life will maximise the time you can spend enjoying life, so make sure you take five or ten minutes every day to plan what you want to do with your 'ME' time and make a list. This will help to keep you focused and you're more likely to stick to your resolution.

Don't call us

When you've set time aside, turn off your mobile phone and leave the answer machine on at home. If the call's not urgent, it can wait.

Give yourself space

How often have you turned down a night out with friends because you 'don't seem to find the time, these days'? Most of us would like to spend more time with our friends and families and do the things that we want to do, when we want to do them. But something called 'life' keeps getting in the way.

No doubt if you've got children you'll spend a great deal of your time cleaning, washing and generally running around picking up after them. With toddlers there's all the toys and clutter they create to deal with, too. No wonder you feel frazzled. But if you put all their stuff into a large storage box at the end of each day, regardless of the fact that it'll be strewn all over the place by nine o'clock the next morning, you'll feel better for it. And start as you mean to go on – teach them to put their own toys and clothes away.

It's not about squeezing more and more into your already hectic schedule. It's about planning how you would like to spend your time so that you can improve the quality of the time available to you.

De-clutter your home

Just stop for a second and take a good long look around your home. What do you see? Is it an ocean of calm? Is it somewhere you can relax and unwind after a long hard day? Are you surrounded by the things you love and treasure – comfortable furnishings, personal trinkets and things that give you pleasure? Or are you steadily drowning in clutter?

If we're honest, we've all got clutter. It's the sort of stuff we poke away in drawers and the back of cupboards telling ourselves that 'it may come in useful, one day'.

Is it time to de-clutter your house?

1. Is there an old scarf or tie you used to wear at university still sitting in your wardrobe, regardless of the fact that you're now 57?
2. Have you got a shoebox of old photos of people you met on holiday but whose names you can't even remember?
3. Is there a box of broken or old toys in the garage?
4. Have you got a box of old music cassettes but nothing to play them on?
5. Is there a pile of unwanted paperbacks cluttering your bookshelves?
6. Is there a folder of articles and recipes cut from magazines sitting in your drawer waiting to be sorted?
7. Is there a shelf of old videos you never play in the living room?

>>

8. Are there any out-of-date herbs and spices in your kitchen?
9. Does your kitchen notice board contain a curled mass of long out-of-date invitations and reminders?
10. Does it take forever to find things in your house?

If you answered 'Yes' to more than three of these questions your house in need of a de-clutter detox.

Clutter is a waste of space, and what's more it's wasting you time as you rummage through the clutter to find something you actually need.

So cut loose, and start again.

A clean sweep

If you approach the clutter mountain gradually and clear one area of the house at a time, it's simple. Every minute you devote to it will lessen the stress and give you more time to devote to the things you want to do.

Getting started can be daunting but once you do, and see the difference even de-cluttering one room can make, you'll be on a roll and licking the rest of the house into shape will seem less intimidating. A tidy, uncluttered house also brings another bonus – cleaning in future will take you less than half the time as you don't have to clear the clutter before you can get started.

Start small

If the thought of de-cluttering your home sends you running for the hills, start by tackling small tasks first. Try setting yourself a ten-minute goal and sort out your underwear drawer. Tip it all out onto the bed; take a good look at each item and ask yourself – do I really want to keep this? If underwear hasn't been worn then pass it on to a charity shop. If you've got three pairs of Bridget Jones-style grey belly-huggers, get rid of them!

One at a time

Tackle one room at a time and don't move to another one until you have de-cluttered and cleaned the first one. Start with a general whip round to chuck out any dead flowers, empty the ashtrays, put dirty cups in the sink and so on. Clean all the surfaces and sweep or vacuum the floors.

Once you've de-cluttered a room, give it a good clean and step back and admire your handiwork. It's a really satisfying feeling and gives you the incentive to move on to the next room.

Keep it up

You've started now, so you might as well carry on! If you need to lift your spirits to face the next task, put on your favourite CD and get stuck in. If you're in an upbeat mood and are feeling good, you're more likely to carry on. Don't get overambitious though and vow to sort out the entire loft, upstairs bedroom and spare room in one morning. Set aside 20 or 30 minutes a day for a task and make sure you stick to it.

Don't go it alone

Get the rest of the family or friends involved. If you absolutely detest that ra-ra skirt you bought when you wanted to look like the lead singer of Bananarama, your friend (or daughter!) may love it. Unwanted items can be passed on to charity shops, friends, family or recycled. Or you could make yourself a bit of money by getting rid of stuff at a car-boot sale. And don't forget selling it on an Internet auction site such as eBay, or through *Loot*'s print magazines or online listings.

Tips for selling on Internet auction sites

- Be precise and accurate in your description, particularly with regard to colour, size, age etc. 'New' must mean exactly that. If an article is worn, describe the wear in detail.
- Photograph your item so it is shown in its best light.
- Be ready to answer any questions from would-be bidders.
- Remember to work out accurately the cost of postage and packing, or you could end up out of pocket.
- If you decide to have a reserve price, be realistic.

Car booting

Taking your unwanted clutter along to a car-boot or table sale can be fun – and it's surprising how much money you can raise.

Here's some tips to have the money rolling in:

- Book your pitch in good time.
- Don't be late. The dealers arrive early in the hope of snapping up the bargains.
- Be selective about what you take. Dump the chipped china, incomplete jigsaws, and books with missing pages.
- Price everything before you leave home but don't be afraid to haggle – people expect it.
- Don't forget some coffee and sandwiches – especially if you

>>

skipped breakfast. Something to sit on during quiet periods is
also a good idea.
- Dress for the weather and take an umbrella – it can double as
a sunshade if it's hot!
- At the end of the sale take everything that hasn't sold to the
charity shop – not back into your house.

Sentimental blues

It's perfectly normal to feel guilty, or even a bit sad, when you're clearing
out personal belongings. You may feel guilty that you're giving away the
hand-knitted shawl your auntie made for you last Christmas, even though
you detest it. Or it may feel wrong, somehow, to get rid of old photos of
drunken people whose names you can't remember. Don't be a slave to
sentiment. It's OK to be sentimental, but you must be selective too. For the
things you really cannot bear to part with, why not put them in a special
keepsakes' box? Or pass on a cherished item to someone you know will
treasure it and give it a good home.

When you're de-cluttering a room, cupboard or drawer, try the three-
bag system.

In bag one: Put all the stuff you want to keep but won't use for
a while. That should go into storage in your loft or garage. You can
then review this in six months' time; if it's still not being used, ask
yourself why you're hanging on to it and if somebody else would
make better use of it.

In bag two: Put all the things you want to repair, reuse or recycle and make sure you get on and do it.

In bag three: Put all the stuff you plan to take to the charity shop or attempt to sell.

Recycle unwanted gifts

There's no polite way to refuse an unwanted gift, but if you really can't stand that china owl ornament with its malevolent red eyes and want to smash it every time you look at it, get rid of it! It'll only drag your spirits down and make you feel miserable every time you see it if you keep it around. Take it to a charity shop or sell it – someone else may love it!

Storage solutions

Invest in storage or, even better, keep cardboard boxes and create your own. Make sure you store like with like and put detailed labels on the boxes, so you don't have to drag them all out to find anything. Keep boxes that you are likely to want to dip into frequently in easily accessible places. It's a good idea to make each of the children a storage box so they can put toys they want to keep, but no longer play with, into 'store'.

Clutter-free Karma

By getting rid of what you don't want or need, you'll enjoy the benefits of a more relaxing, stress-free home. You'll be able to find what you need when you need it. You won't need to rush around frantically shovelling things in drawers to hide the mess when unexpected visitors arrive. You'll no longer have to greet guests with the immortal words: 'Lovely to see you. Please, excuse the mess.' And you'll be making the best use of space in your home, too.

> Don't dither – deal with it. Did you know that most bits of paper get picked up 10 to 20 times before they're dealt with?

Be a creative de-junker
● Make a giant collage with your best and funniest photos or old post-cards; paste them to a board and put them in a large clip-frame. That way you can enjoy them every day and make them a feature of your home.
● If something's broken or you simply can't stand to look at it, get rid of it. You should only have things around you that you love and that make you feel good.
● Invest in some coat hooks and a shoe rack near the front door for coats, shoes and bags, so that when you're all tearing about in the mornings and are rushing to leave the house you can just grab stuff and go.

Get a clean routine
Once you've conquered the clutter, it's time to devise a cleaning routine that works for you. It's easy to see what the major cleaning jobs are in our homes, so it's best to leave those for when you have time to do them.

Having said that, don't let things build up so that when you get around to cleaning them they're so grubby it takes a day and a half to get them back to their former glory. The best way to develop a routine is to divide your cleaning into manageable tasks.

- Things that need a daily clean
- Things that need a regular clean
- Things that need an occasional clean
- Stuff that needs to be blitzed once a year

Let in some fresh air!

Closed windows provide insulation and stop us wasting heat – but it shouldn't mean you end up living in a hermetically sealed box. Household pests such as dust mites thrive in warm, humid atmospheres. So it's time to fling open the windows.

Case Study
The Cunningham-Locke's

Dad Jeff, Mum Caroline and their children Chloe aged 7, Rhys (6) and foster daughter Karen (12).

The Cunningham-Locke's back garden was strewn with building gear, toys and general rubbish. The loft was going to be cleared to prepare it for insulation, but it was crammed with stuff they hadn't even looked at in years and that meant they had to get to grips with some serious de-cluttering.

Rather than sending it all to landfill, a local recycling company was called and they dropped off a skip. The family put all the things they no longer needed — which included toys, electrical equipment, wood and clothing — into the skip. There was a cost of £180, but the recycling company then sorted out the various items and sent them for reuse, repair or, if the item was beyond repair, appropriate disposal.

With a clear loft and garden, the Cunningham-Locke's were able to make use of valuable space that had been lost to them. They also painted their lounge with an eco-friendly paint and managed to finish jobs they had been putting off for ages.

It was not the calmest of homes — Dad was addicted to his stereo, Rhys to his computer games and the girls to the TV. With so much noise and distraction there was a lot of shouting, mostly because they couldn't hear what anyone else was saying. The solution? A ration on the amount of time the TV, games and stereo could be on. At first the family were horrified and wondered what they would do with their time.

But as they began to do more as a family — play games, get some jobs out of the way and, yes, talk — things got better. Just one week later, the house was definitely a more relaxing place to be. They had worked as a team and found that talking and listening without the distraction of all that white noise was interesting and pleasurable.

De-cluttering really does add to the quality of our day-to-day life. A solid weekend of work, cracking through that list of jobs, brings something priceless — a sense of calm and achievement.

TOP FIVE TIPS

1. Make each member of the family responsible for their own de-junking.
2. Re-cycle as much as you can by donating unwanted items to charity shops or by selling them.
3. Tidy before you clean, it saves so much time.
4. Tidy the kitchen after you finish cooking and the sitting room before you go to bed.
5. Reserve a portion of 'me' time every day.

What you have saved . . .

● A tidy sum from selling your junk – for example, old records can make you a few bob on eBay, electrical items can be sold in Loot and everyone can make something from a car-boot sale.
● Time and lots of it – more efficient time-planning could save you an hour a day, seven hours a week, 365 hours a year. . .
● Your sanity – you've made way for peace and quiet in your home.

USEFUL CONTACTS

The best-known Internet auction site is **eBay** – their UK site is at www.ebay.co.uk.

You can place adverts in *Loot*'s print magazines, or on their website, at www.loot.com.

6
The clean, green home

The air quality in your home can be five times more polluted than the outside air. It may come as a shock to learn that our homes are filled with a potentially poisonous cocktail of chemicals that can cause serious health problems. Good air quality is vital for our health, and most of us tend to spend approximately 90 per cent of our time indoors.

We all need a constant supply of clean, fresh air to live and to maintain our health but, because of our wasteful ways, we're polluting the air with car exhaust fumes, chemicals from factories producing our consumer goods, and power stations generating our energy supply.

The air that we breathe

A certain amount of indoor air pollution is simply outdoor pollution that has found its way into our homes. But what exactly is air pollution? Air is considered to be polluted if it contains substances which could damage our health and the environment or which cause a nuisance. And according to some experts, pollution can be worse indoors than outdoors. Yet good air quality indoors is often overlooked as a means of improving our quality of life.

Does anyone in your household regularly suffer from:

- Headaches
- Itchy or watering eyes, or nose
- Throat infections
- Dizziness
- Nausea
- Frequent colds
- Asthma
- Bronchitis

Although you should always consult your doctor if you are worried about any symptoms of illness, the symptoms above could well indicate high levels of indoor air pollution.

Many symptoms relating to indoor air pollution follow a seasonal pattern. For example, you may notice that yours and your family's symptoms are worse when the building is tightly sealed during winter, or when the weather is hot and humid in summer. Symptoms may also occur when you're doing a major spring clean, or decorating.

The first step towards improving indoor air quality should be to remove or reduce, where possible, as many sources of pollutants and toxins as you can.

Potentially harmful chemicals can be found in anything from soft furnishings, carpets and paints to household cleaning products, toiletries and cosmetics. And these toxins can accumulate inside your home without you even realising they are there.

It's a gas

There are believed to be up to 300 volatile organic compounds (VOCs) inside the typical home. These chemicals are generated from household cleaning products, paints, building materials, furnishings, carpets and tobacco smoke. VOCs are carcinogenic, so long-term exposure to certain VOCs can lead to an increased risk of various cancers.

MDF, veneered chipboard or plywood furniture emits toxic chemicals, but if you buy solid wood furniture, it's unlikely to give off harmful chemicals. Carpets and soft furnishings are also responsible for giving off chemicals such as formaldehyde.

Formaldehyde isn't just something trendy artists use to pickle dead sheep! This chemical is a VOC that can be found in any number of house-hold items, including foam insulation, chipboard furniture and emulsion paints. High concentrations of formaldehyde can lead to eye and airway irritation, neurological damage, asthma and cancer.

Carbon monoxide is another hidden danger in our homes. This gas is colourless and odourless – and toxic. It's produced by the incomplete combustion of fossil fuels such as natural gas, propane, heating oil, paraffin, coal, charcoal, petrol or wood. Any appliance that depends on burning these fuels for energy or heat such as gas fires, central-heating boilers, room heaters, water heaters, cookers or grills can produce carbon monoxide if they are not installed, maintained or used correctly.

Because you can't see or smell carbon monoxide, it has no warning properties and is often called 'the silent killer'. Initial symptoms of exposure may include dizziness, excessive tiredness and fatigue, headaches, nausea and irregular breathing. However, death from poisoning can occur without any of these symptoms being experienced – a person may simply fall asleep and fail to regain consciousness.

Plants – the ultimate green machines

Plants are the oldest, most natural air filters on the planet. There are a number of common house plants that have been shown to effectively detox households by absorbing poisonous vapours and releasing oxygen back into the air. A great source for helping to find plant puri-fiers is www.flowers.org.uk. Species to look out for include Mexican cacti, spider plants, ivy, rubber plants and gerbera daisies, which are all said to help humidify and freshen up stale environments.

Allergic to your house?

Pollen, dust, cleaning products, cosmetics and toiletries, pets, etc. Your house is full of substances that can cause allergies and sensitivities in certain people.

By reducing your use of suspect chemicals, and keeping pets and flowers away from sensitive individuals, you can do a lot to reduce their suffering.

House-dust mites are tiny, microscopic creatures that live in carpets, bedding and soft furnishings and are believed to be one of the major triggers for asthma and eczema. Mites like warm, damp conditions, so regular vacuum cleaning and high-temperature washing of clothes when necessary can help control their numbers.

Dust-mite excrement can build up in mattresses, duvets and pillows: according to some experts, 70 per cent of the weight of your pillow is likely to be dust mite droppings. Use a steam cleaner on mattresses to kill the bugs without using chemicals.

Pet subject

Despite Britain being a nation of animal lovers, loads of people are allergic to cats and dogs, as their hair, fur and dander from their coats can trigger allergies in susceptible people and can make existing conditions such as asthma worse.

To keep pet allergens at a minimum, make certain rooms pet-free zones and remember to wash and groom pets regularly. The Cat Protection League and Canine Defence League can provide you with tips on how to make life easier for anyone with allergies or asthma exacerbated by pets.

Or contact the Asthma UK advice line on 08457 010203 (www.asthma.
org.uk).

There's also a product called Petal Cleanse which removes allergens
from the coat (www.bio-life.co.uk).

> House dust is made up of a disgusting mixture of dirt, pet hair,
> dust-mite excrement and flakes of human hair and skin.

It's getting damp in here

Water vapour is produced when we cook or take a bath or shower.
Condensation can build up in our homes thanks to warm, wet air
produced in kitchens or bathrooms being allowed to circulate around
the house to unheated rooms such as bedrooms, where the moisture
condenses.

In these conditions, mould may start to grow. And apart from being
damaging and unsightly, mould can produce spores that can aggravate
chest complaints and respiratory conditions such as asthma and bronchitis when inhaled.

Anti-damp tips:

● Fit mechanical extractor fans, preferably fitted with a humidistat, to
kitchens or bathrooms where a lot of moist air is produced.

● Keep kitchen and bathroom doors closed to prevent dampness
spreading to other parts of the home.

● Keep rooms well aired and try to avoid condensation by opening
windows in bathrooms to let moist air escape after a bath.

● Keep lids on saucepans when cooking to keep moisture under control.

- Ensure your home is properly insulated and heated; you may need a low level of heating even in unused rooms to stop condensation occurring.

If you spot mould, this is a definite symptom of dampness, so to get rid of it you need to get to the root of the problem and cure the dampness first.

If you know what's causing the damp then, once that's been remedied, you can clean and treat mould spots and redecorate, if necessary, using an anti-mould paint. If you can't work out what's causing dampness, speak to your local authority's Environmental Health Officer.

Cleaning ourselves to death?

None of us can totally avoid coming into contact with chemicals: for better or for worse they have become a part of our everyday lives. While we know that things like drain cleaners and bleach could, if swallowed, be extremely bad for our health, we regularly spray and slather all kinds of toxic potions around our homes.

For example, there are a whole host of potentially harmful chemicals in some of the most popular household cleaning products, cosmetics and toiletries — we just don't expect them to be there.

Organisations like Friends of the Earth, Greenpeace and the Women's Environmental Network have identified various chemicals used in household products as being particularly risky and detrimental to our health — a large proportion of them can disrupt our hormone function.

Perhaps even more worrying is the fact that some of these chemicals are persistent, taking years and years to break down. This means they can accumulate – once they're there, they stay there.

No one wants their home to smell of damp dogs, last night's take-away curry and cheesy football socks. We all want our houses to be spick and span, our whites to be 'brilliant whites', and for indoors to smell like the summer meadows outdoors.

But, hang on. What kind of Stepford Wives fantasy is this? Have you ever read the label on the back of your furniture polish? Do you know what makes your whites 'whiter-than-white'? That's right – chemicals. And do you know what those chemicals do to the environment, and your health?

We assume that if a product is available in the supermarket and is on sale to the public, it's got to be safe. And we love the added benefit of lots of praise about how lovely our homes are when people come to visit. However, in pursuing this picture-perfect existence, we may be cleaning ourselves to death.

If the label said 'POISON' in big black letters, and had a skull and crossbones as its logo, you wouldn't buy it. But because it promises gleaming dust-free surfaces and cleaner dishes, you'll happily load up your supermarket trolley with the stuff.

We need to become more label aware.

Jargon buster
- Persistent chemicals – chemicals that enter the environment or our bodies and don't break down easily.
- Bio-accumulative – when persistent chemicals build up in body tissues such as fat.

>>

>>

- Endocrine disrupters – chemicals that have adverse effects on hormones in the body, particularly oestrogen.

Learning the labels

The 'ingredients lists' on household cleaning products aren't as comprehensive as those on foods. Manufacturers don't have to list all the ingredients in cleaning products, they simply have to state whether something is harmful or not.

Orange and black hazard symbols tell you what the main dangers are and should be read along with the risk phrase or safety phrase.

- A risk phrase is typically a standard safety warning about using the product, for example, 'risk of serious damage to eyes'.
- Safety phrases tell you about the precautions you need to take when using and storing a product, for example, 'use only in a well-ventilated area'.

Harmful or irritant
Black cross on an orange background
Products with these symbols contain substances that can cause harm to human health, and damage skin or internal membranes.

Flammable or extremely flammable
Fire in an orange square
Many aerosols carry one of these symbols, so keep them away from naked flames and don't put them on the bonfire.

Toxic or very toxic
Skull and crossbones
These products are poisonous if consumed. Be careful not to inhale or swallow these products or spill them on your skin, where they could be absorbed.

Corrosive
Drops of liquid burning through a hand
This literally does what it says on the tin – if the product comes into contact with your skin or is swallowed it will destroy living tissue.

Tactile danger warnings
These raised triangle shapes warn people who have difficulty seeing the orange-and-black symbols. It can be easily felt by fingertips and is either embossed on the container or takes the form of a raised transparent sticker.

Solvent abuse can kill instantly
The use of this statement is voluntary, so you won't find it on every product that poses this risk. It normally appears as a separate warning on many solvent-containing products such as aerosols and spray adhesive.

Child resistant
Products must have child-resistant closures (lids, caps, etc.) on any products labelled 'very toxic', 'toxic' or 'corrosive'. There is also a list of specific chemicals that, if used as an ingredient, automatically means a manufacturer must use child-resistant packaging. However, these

closures don't necessarily mean that the product is childproof – you can't be sure your child won't figure them out – so keep all such products out of the reach of children.

Other labelling

Since 1989 there has been an EU recommendation on ingredient labelling for detergent and cleaning products. Certain ingredients should, therefore, be labelled if they're present in the product in a concentration of 0.2 per cent or more. Enzymes, preservatives and optical brighteners (found in some washing powders) should be labelled regardless of their concentrations.

The full name, address and telephone number of the manufacturer must also be printed on all dangerous products.

The chemical cocktail inside us all

A recent study found that each of us is typically walking around with more than 300 man-made compounds in our bodies. Nobody knows what long-term effects these chemicals will have on our health, so it pays to know what the main culprits are and how we're exposed to them. Once we know what they are and how they get inside us, we can minimise our use of them.

Phthalates

These are a group of chemicals strongly suspected of being hormone disruptors. Their main use is to make certain plastics flexible and can be found in some plastic food wrapping. Several of the worst phthalates have been banned from children's toys, but Greenpeace believes the legislation isn't enough, and warns people not to give anything made from PVC or vinyl to babies.

Phthalates are also used as ingredients in many beauty products, and some baby toiletries also contain phthalates.

Bisphenol A

This is another endocrine-disrupting chemical found in polycarbonate plastics, which are used to make baby feeding bottles, water bottles and food storage containers, and in the lining of food tins. Most baby feeding bottles sold in the UK are made from polycarbonate plastic derived from Bisphenol A, but manufacturers say that polycarbonate bottles are safer to use than glass feeding bottles, which can break.

Artificial musks

These are used in a variety of fragranced products, such as washing powders, cosmetics, air fresheners and shower gels. For instance, many air fresheners contain hormone-disrupting artificial musks (sometimes loosely referred to as 'parfum' on the label). You'll also find artificial musks in some baby creams, wipes and other cosmetic products and toiletries.

Alkylphenols

These are used in detergents, paints, glues and lubricating oils as well as in some cosmetics, from shampoos to shaving foams. Alkylphenols become more endocrine-disrupting in the environment when they break down. These breakdown products have been found to cause reproductive problems in fish and river creatures, and have been linked to human fertility problems.

Organotins

These are also known as alkyltins and are used in the production of about 8 per cent of PVC products produced in Europe, and also as an anti-bacterial and anti-fungal agent, for example in anti-bacterial insoles for shoes. Organotins have also been detected in disposable nappies.

Fortunately there are some responsible manufacturers out there, so you do have a choice. To help you, Friends of the Earth provides a list of all the major high-street retailers who were prepared to respond to a questionnaire on the safety of their products. Visit www.foe.co.uk/resource/reports/ shop_till_you_drop.pdf to see the full results.

Getting rid of hazardous rubbish

By now you know that the golden rules are to Reduce, Reuse and Recycle wherever possible. However, there are a number of household hazards that just aren't practical to treat in this way, and need to be disposed of carefully.

Up to 5 per cent of household waste can be classed as hazardous due to its potential to harm human health and the environment. The following information should help you to identify the major hazardous materials and dispose of them safely.

Start by reducing your waste

Once you know which chemicals and products are the most dangerous, you can minimise the amount of hazardous waste you generate by avoiding or minimising your use of them, by buying materials you know are less hazardous or by using alternatives.

- Buy paints, varnishes, glues, and cleaning and treatment agents that are plant-based, water-based or low in solvents rather than chemical-based versions.
- Buy more long-lasting products such as rechargeable batteries – don't go for disposables where you can help it.
- Always follow the usage and disposal instructions, and use only as much as you need. Many people use far too much of cleaning products such as washing-up liquid.
- Follow the safe disposal instructions (where applicable) to the letter.
- Donate unwanted or broken furniture and fridges or freezers to charities and community organisations that repair and redistribute them.

Oils

Motor oil – if you do your own oil changes, your unwanted engine oil needs to be disposed of very carefully. In fact, it's illegal to pour it down the drain and if you're caught you could be given a hefty fine. That's not surprising when you consider that the oil from one car oil change can pollute the surface of a lake the size of two football pitches.

Unwanted oil can be recycled and purified for reuse, so you can take unwanted engine oil to a local garage that operates a recycling scheme, or contact your local authority recycling officer for further advice.

The Environment Agency runs an Oil Care campaign, which will give you information on the nearest recycling facility or garage recycling scheme. Visit their website at www.oilbankline.org.uk or contact them on 08708 506 506.

Cooking oil – oil and melted fat shouldn't be disposed of by pouring it down the sink as it can block the drains and attract vermin such as rats. Contact the Environment Agency for further information.

You could save up the waste fat to mix with seeds, nuts and raisins to make a 'bird cake' to help feed the birds in your garden in winter.

Shock statistics

- It only takes one litre of oil to pollute one million litres of fresh drinking water.
- Waste oil from nearly three million car oil changes in Britain is not collected; if collected properly, this could meet the annual energy needs of 1.5 million people.

Paint

Although not strictly hazardous waste, household paints contain VOCs, which can be harmful to human health if substantial amounts are inhaled, and can damage the environment if they're not disposed of correctly.

Paints or paint thinners should not be poured down drains. If you have small quantities of residual paint then it's best if you just allow it to dry out naturally (somewhere people won't inhale the fumes) or use old newspaper to soak up any excess. The paint containers can then be disposed of at your local recycling centre – but check with your local authority first, as these facilities may not be available at your standard recycling drop-off point.

If you've got larger quantities of paint that you no longer need, then you can donate them to a Community RePaint scheme. This network of paint reuse schemes offers a free collection service and distributes reusable paints free of charge to charities, voluntary organisations, community sector groups and public agencies. You can find more information at www.communityrepaint.org.uk.

For more about environmentally friendly paints, see chapter 8.

Fridges and freezers

Fridges and freezers contain chemicals that deplete the ozone layer, so they have to be disposed of responsibly. Local authorities are obliged by law to provide facilities for householders to dispose of unwanted fridges and freezers. Usually, they will collect the appliances and dispose of them safely, though they are allowed to charge a fee for this service. Alternatively, you can take your old fridge or freezer to your local civic amenity and recycling site. Contact your local authority for further details.

Many community or charity organisations will collect fridges and freezers free of charge, if they are in good working order. Or contact the Furniture Reuse Network (www.frn.org.uk) and ask about their fridge collection service, which guarantees that up to 15 per cent of the units donated will be reused and passed on to low-income families.

Batteries

Most batteries contain heavy metals and only a very small percentage of consumer-disposable batteries are recycled – most end up in landfill sites.

Some local authorities collect household batteries as part of their multi-material kerbside collection schemes, so it makes sense to check first with the local authority recycling officer to see what's available in your area.

REBAT (www.rebat.com) will collect most types of portable rechargeable batteries in the UK for recycling. In addition, some retailers and DIY shops have battery collection points near their stores. Rechargeable batteries can also be recycled once they have reached the end of their useful lives.

Medicines

If you're rummaging in your bathroom cabinets and drawers and find any boxes, jars or bottles of medicines and pharmaceutical products that have passed their use-by dates or are no longer needed, dispose of them correctly.

Although these are obviously not safe to take, old medicines should never be thrown away with your normal rubbish or put down the sink or toilet. All unwanted medicines should be kept in their original packaging and taken back to the chemist, who will dispose of them safely for you.

Asbestos

Asbestos is a substance that, when inhaled, can cause serious lung damage, and long-term exposure can cause cancer.

Asbestos was once used in all kinds of household materials such as insulation, roofing and in appliances such as cookers and electric blankets. New legislation introduced in 2006 means it can't be used any more, so you'll only find it in older buildings or in outbuildings such as garages and garden sheds. If the asbestos is damaged and released during building, renovation or when you call in an electrician, plumber, etc., this can be hazardous to the health of all involved.

Working with, and disposing of, asbestos requires special, very stringent safety precautions, and this MUST be left to the experts. If you discover that your house insulation, for example, contains asbestos, you should contact your local authority waste disposal officer.

Asbestos-related health problems are almost always 'industrial diseases', found in people who have worked with the substance in the past.

Green cleaning products

Women are being encouraged by organisations such as the Women's Environmental Network to minimise waste and to use more environmentally friendly products in the home. Good sources of these products are The Green Shop at www.greenshop.co.uk, Earth Friendly Products (www.greenbrands.co.uk) and Ecover products (www.ecover.com and from some supermarkets).

Laundry borax

Laundry borax is very effective as an antibacterial, cleaning, fungicidal and bleaching agent. If you replace your usual household cleaning products with borax it's better for your health and the environment. It can be used for a wide range of household cleaning jobs instead of chemical cleaners — here are just a few to try:

>>

>>

- Add half a cup of borax to your washing with the usual amount of washing powder to boost its cleaning power and deodorise the wash.
- Soak delicates in a solution of one or two tablespoons of washing powder and a quarter-cup of borax in a bowl of warm water. Rinse in cool water and dry.
- Dissolve one tablespoon of borax in a litre of warm water and use the solution to wipe the fridge clean and deodorise it at the same time.
- For wine and other liquid stains on carpets, dissolve half a cup of borax in half a litre of warm water, leave for half an hour and sponge off. For odours, dampen the area, then sprinkle with borax. Leave to dry and then vacuum.

Borax can be purchased from Wilkinsons, Robert Dyas, local hardware stores and chemist shops, as well as The Green Shop and other eco-friendly retailers.

Note: Although borax is a natural substance, you should always wear gloves when using it as it can irritate the skin. Take extreme care with the storage of borax, particularly if there are children or pets in the house. Do **not** use boric acid – this is an entirely different substance.

Green cleaning recipes

If you don't want to spend money replacing your household cleaning products with manufactured eco-friendly ones, then why not try some timeless, natural alternatives to the usual chemical cocktails? They stood Granny in good stead for years, and they'll save you money as well.

Here's how to use some of the products that you may already have in your kitchen cupboards.

Kitchen bins

Kitchen bins should be emptied frequently – and well before the contents start to smell. Wash them out once a week. You could try using a solution of one teaspoon of borax in 500ml of hot water as a disinfectant, rather than swilling it round with bleach. Alternatively, thyme oil and salt both have disinfectant properties.

Kitchen cupboards

Kitchen cupboards should be cleaned out regularly – several times a year. Take out all the food from each cupboard and throw away any items that are past their sell-by date. Then, wash the interior of the cupboards with a solution of bicarbonate of soda and warm water and wipe dry with an old towel. Leave the cupboard for a couple of hours to dry thoroughly before restocking with the food.

Freezers

The more you open the door of your freezer, the more you'll need to defrost it (and the more energy you'll waste as the cold air escapes). As a general rule, you should defrost your freezer when the ice reaches a thickness of 5mm. When defrosting is finished, dry the interior then rinse with a solution of bicarbonate of soda (15ml of soda to 1 litre of water), and dry with a clean towel. If smells still linger, fill the freezer with crumpled newspapers and leave it switched off with the door slightly open for a couple of days. Newspaper helps to absorb smells.

Fridges

Fridges need to be washed regularly to keep them fresh. Clear out all of the food and remove the shelves. Wash the interior with the same bicarbonate of soda solution mentioned above. Shelves and other bits and bobs can be washed in a solution of warm water and borax.

Once or twice a year, make sure you pull the fridge away from the wall and dust the coils at the back to remove dust build-up, as this will make your fridge less energy efficient and add pounds to your electricity bills.

Ovens

A paste of baking soda and water left on for five minutes and then washed off with a scouring cloth and hot water makes an effective oven cleaner. Sprinkle salt on spills while they are still warm to ease cleaning once the oven is cool.

Kettles

Furry deposits can build up on kettle elements – especially in hard-water areas. It's best to de-scale kettles before the fur has had a chance to build up. Distilled white vinegar is good for removing scaly deposits in kettles (as well as limescale in toilets, baths and sinks). And if you use a teapot, then lemon juice is good for removing tea stains.

Bathrooms

Limescale build-up and blue-green marks on enamel baths are a sure sign that you've got a constantly dripping tap. So, first things first, you need to get that fixed, as you're wasting water. To get rid of stubborn stains, use bicarbonate of soda to scour sinks and baths and to treat tidemarks. Mouldy areas that appear around bath sealant can be treated with a solution of borax and then scrubbed with an old toothbrush.

Blocked drains
Dissolve a quarter of a cup of baking soda and 50ml of vinegar in boiling water and use to unblock drains.

Tiles
Wipe over with a white-vinegar solution (one part vinegar to four parts water), then rinse and wipe dry.

Toilets
Regular brushing and flushing and a once-a-week clean with borax should be sufficient for loos. Bleach damages the ceramic glaze of the pan and makes the loo more difficult to clean. Hard-water build-up should be covered with a thick paste of borax and vinegar, left for a couple of hours, then brushed off and rinsed.

Showers
If shower curtains are prone to mildew, soak them in vinegar and water and then rinse and machine wash (check the label first). Hard-water deposits on shower walls can be treated with neat white vinegar – leave for 15 minutes and rinse off.

If your showerhead is clogged, soak all the pieces (apart from the rubber washer) in neat white malt vinegar. Use an old toothbrush to brush away sediment build-up and chalky deposits before putting it back together again.

Windows

Try using two tablespoons of white vinegar and some borax in a spray bottle for cleaning windows. Some smearing may occur on first use due to waxy build-up from previous spray cleaners, but the borax will help to remove this.

Laundry

Soak grubby whites in a 5 per cent dilution of lemon juice and water and leave outside in the sunlight. Then add 30ml of bicarbonate of soda to the washing water and a squirt of lemon juice in the rinse for glorious whites. If black clothes have faded to murky grey, soak them in warm water with a little vinegar added to restore them.

If the clothes you've been wearing during the day are not dirty, they could still do with an airing before you put them away, as all clothes tend to pick up smells. Hang your clothes up by the shower or preferably outside for a couple of hours to refresh them. This will help your clothes to last much longer, too, as they won't be constantly knocked about in the washing machine.

Note: If you make your own household cleaners remember to keep them in secure containers clearly labelled with the contents. Keep them out of reach of children.

Case Study
The Lambert Family

Peter, wife Karen, mum-in-law Pam, and daughters Jade (19) and Krystle (21).

Peter is the only man in the Lambert household, sharing the home with four women who drive him mad with their constant use of hair and beauty gizmos and gadgets — which they always forget to turn off. Their electricity bill was nearly three times more than the national average.

You certainly couldn't fault the Lamberts' attention to cleanliness — but they racked up a long list of unnecessary consumer products to maintain their pristine lifestyle. Karen and Pam were perhaps a little over-obsessed with the house being immaculate and smelling nice. The washing machine was on for 18 hours a week on average, and they used the vacuum cleaner for 30 minutes a day. Plug-in air fresheners were found in every room. They also liked the house to be unbearably hot — the heating was on 24/7 (partly because Pete didn't know how to use the timer).

Krystle loved wearing the latest fashions, wouldn't be seen dead in the same outfit twice, and wouldn't dream of answering the door without her make-up on. Rather than recycle her clothes, she'd bin them and buy new ones. As a member of the cabin crew of a budget airline, she's also clocking up the air miles — polluting the air with even more fumes! And Peter's prized possession is his Jacuzzi, which he was heating to 39 degrees, for all hours of the day — ready for him to jump into every morning for his hour-long soak.

It was plain that the whole family had to cut down on household products — and they started with changing the way they cleaned. Karen and Pam de-cluttered their kitchen cupboards, which were stuffed with cleaning products containing polluting and potentially harmful chemicals. From now on, they would use old-fashioned remedies for cleaning, such as vinegar, newspaper, salt, lemons and bicarbonate of soda – all of which Pam had used years ago.

The family were delighted with the results and eventually weaned themselves off all of their toxic products. They even replaced all those plug-in air fresheners with home-made potpourri.

Poisoning: what to do in an emergency

All medicines, cleaning products, garden chemicals, etc., must always be stored in a safe place where children and pets can't get to them. It's good practice to regularly review your storage arrangements to make sure that harmful substances are kept safely out of reach.

Heaven forbid that anyone in your house should actually ingest anything that's poisonous – but unfortunately accidents do happen. If someone in your house does swallow something toxic, this is what you should do.

● Give them frequent sips of water if they have swallowed a corrosive liquid such as bleach.
● If they're unconscious, check that the airway is clear of vomit and tilt the head backwards.
● If they're breathing but unconscious, put them in the recovery position.

>>

- Do not induce vomiting – if a substance burns going down, it will burn coming back up, and do even more damage.
- For an inhaled poison, take the person into the open air.

The recovery position

- Turn the casualty onto their side.
- Lift the chin forwards to open the airway and adjust the hand under the cheek as necessary.
- Check that the casualty cannot roll forwards or backwards.
- Monitor the casualty's breathing and pulse continuously.
- If injuries allow, turn the casualty to the other side after 30 minutes.

For a baby less than a year old, a modified recovery position must be adopted: cradle the infant in your arms, with their head tilted downwards to prevent them from choking on their tongue or inhaling vomit.

Monitor and record vital signs – level of response, pulse and breathing – until medical help arrives.

It's a good idea to attend a first-aid course, so that you know what to do in an emergency, and to practise techniques such as putting someone into the recovery position.

Always seek medical advice immediately if you suspect poisoning.

How ugly are your beauty products?

- Would you rub chemicals into your wrinkles?
- Would you brush your teeth with washing liquid?
- Would you put petroleum on your hair?

Remember, every product you put on your body is made up of chemical ingredients, and some of these chemicals are believed to have harmful effects on our health. Some are thought to be toxic, while others could be endocrine-disrupters, which mess up our hormone systems.

A proportion of the products we apply to our faces, bodies and hair are absorbed through our skin.

Scientists are still unsure of the exact health implications, but it's safe to say we could all do with cutting down the amount of synthetic chemicals we douse our bodies with.

Open your bathroom cupboards, look on your dressing tables and empty your gym bags. Many people use twenty different personal products on a daily basis. People in the UK spend nearly six billion pounds on personal care every year. Not only could we be harming ourselves with the chemicals we're using, we are flushing these chemicals down the drain and into the sea, where they can build up in the environment and cause damage.

Many people prefer not to use toothpastes containing fluoride, particularly for small children (who often swallow their paste!). In fact, most toothpastes recommend they are kept out of the reach of children, and that they should only use a pea-sized amount and be supervised when using it. Many brands now produce non-fluoride toothpaste. Weleda (www.weleda.co.uk) is one of the best known, but with a little careful shopping you can find other brands on supermarkets and chemists' shelves. And whatever toothpaste you use, you can help keep your teeth healthy with regular brushing and flossing, and avoiding sugary foods and drinks, especially between meals.

What can you do?

The best advice for buying beauty products packed with chemicals is to strip down every claim of the advertising.

- Do you really need a separate product to do this job?
- Would a natural ingredient do just as good a job?
- 'Hypoallergenic' doesn't provide an absolute guarantee that you won't have an allergic reaction.
- Sometimes products are marketed as 'natural' or containing 'organic' ingredients – when in fact they only contain small amounts of 'green' ingredients, but plenty of nastier ones. Are you being conned?

Don't drink the water!

Pure water does not contain any toxins, but over the past fifty years our drinking water has had more and more additives incorporated into the mains supply in order to make it safe. These may spoil the taste, but they rarely cause anything more than extremely minor health problems.

Alternatives to drinking tap water:
- Drink bottled water – but this can be expensive.

- Filter your water – you can buy special active-carbon filters, which work by removing chemicals as they pass through, and can be plumbed in under the kitchen sink or attached to the end of a kitchen tap.
- Alternatively, you can use a simple jug filter – a plastic lid containing an active-carbon filter fits on top of the jug and filters the water as it is poured through.

Avoid drinking from the hot tap. Hot water is usually stored in a plastic or metal tank, and as water is a natural corrosive the surrounding material may well have seeped into it.

POTENTIAL SAVINGS
You could save up to £30 a month (£360 a year) by using natural cleaning and beauty products.

TOP FIVE TIPS
1. Keep your house well ventilated, particularly when painting or decorating.
2. Minimise your use of chemical cleaners – try to use natural alternatives.
3. Always dispose of household chemicals safely.
4. Use a vacuum cleaner with a special filter to remove house-dust mites and other allergens.
5. Try to use toiletries and cosmetics that don't rely on petrochemicals and other potentially harmful or irritant ingredients.

USEFUL CONTACTS

For information on asthma, try **Asthma UK** (www.asthma.org.uk), contact their advice line on 08457 010203 or visit their website.

For information on pet allergies, contact **Cats Protection** (www.cats.org.uk), or the **Dogs Trust** (www.dogstrust.org.uk).

Petal Cleanse (www.bio-life.co.uk) produces allergen-removing lotions for use on pets.

Allergy UK (www.allergyuk.org) is the leading medical charity for people with allergy, intolerance and chemical sensitivity. Call their help line on 01322 619898.

Friends of the Earth (www.foe.co.uk) is a great source of information on toxic chemicals in the home, along with other environmental issues.

Recycle your motor oil through the Environment Agency's Oil Care campaign. Visit their website at www.oilbankline.org.uk or contact them on 08708 506506 to find your nearest recycling facility or garage recycling scheme.

Community RePaint (www.communityrepaint.org.uk) is a network of paint reuse schemes.

REBAT (www.rebat.com) will collect and recycle certain kinds of batteries.

You can buy green cleaning products from **The Green Shop** (www.greenshop.co.uk), **Earth Friendly Products** (www.greenbrands.co.uk) and **Ecover** (www.ecover.com and from some supermarkets).

The **Women's Environmental Network** (www.wen.org.uk) has information on green cleaning products, and the health hazards posed by chemicals in our homes.

7
Grow a greener garden

Do you apply the three 'Rs' to the outside space you're responsible for?

Even if you're not lucky enough to have a garden, you might still have some outside space you can call your own – even if it's just a balcony or a few plant pots on the windowsill. There are plenty of things you can do to cut down on waste and become a bit more 'green' fingered.

How green is your gardening?

How far along the green garden path are you? Answer yes or no to the questions in this quiz to find out.

1. I grow some fruit, vegetables or herbs.
2. I don't use chemicals in the garden.
3. I have a wormery to compost vegetable waste.
4. I have a compost heap.
5. I use a water butt to conserve rainwater.
6. I use 'grey' water to water my garden.
7. I mulch my flowerbeds to conserve moisture in the ground.
8. I grow plants that attract insects and birds into my garden.

Count the number of questions you answered with 'yes'.
Score:

1–3 You're on the green path but you have some way left to go.

4–6 You're getting there, not much further to go.

6–8 Congratulations, you've got the green gardening message.

Grow your own

If you really want to avoid the supermarkets and shops – or at least reduce the amount you rely on them – then why not grow some of your own food?

Of course, growing your own food takes a bit of time and effort, but what's more important than your health, and the health of the planet? Good, wholesome, home-grown food is just one way of ensuring that we're not filling up our bodies with the pre-processed muck that we so often grab in the shops because it's there, or because it'll save us time. You can also ensure that your fruit and vegetables are organically grown.

Allotments

If you haven't got a garden, think about an allotment. These are normally administered by your local council, and you can rent a plot of land to grow all sorts of crops on, and they are extremely cheap. For example, you can grow potatoes, corn on the cob, runner beans and all sorts of currants and berries, etc. It's a good way of getting to know other people in your local community, too.

Growing your own food takes time, and can be hard work. If you don't fancy doing all the hard work yourself, why not share it with friends and/or family. Shared allotments are on the increase and mean that when you go on holiday, someone else can water your plants.

An allotment costs around £30 a year to rent. And your fruit and vegetables will have no packaging, there will be no queues at the checkout, and no unknown chemicals sprayed on your food.

Allotments are very trendy right now, and you may find you have to join a waiting list before you get your own plot of land. Be patient – the wait will be worth it!

> At harvest time there is nothing so rewarding as sharing your glut of good home-grown food with friends, neighbours and family.

Growing in small spaces

If space is limited, or if you live in a flat, you can grow a surprising amount of food on a windowsill or in containers.

It's easy to grow herbs in pots on a windowsill. They will need regular feeding and watering and you must be prepared to change them regularly as you use them up, or if they die back. Herbs can also be grown in hanging baskets and window baskets, so this is another alternative for you.

Sweet peppers, chillies, tomatoes, strawberries and 'cut-and-come-again' salad leaves can also be grown on a windowsill.

If you live in a flat with a balcony, container vegetable growing is a really good way to grow your own food. If space is really limited, go for climbing plants, such as French or runner beans or peas. Don't waste time and effort on root crops like beetroot, turnip or things such as cabbage – instead go for vegetables with shallow roots like lettuce, tomatoes or spring onions.

Pots and containers dry out quickly on sunny days, so you'll need to keep them well watered and fed.

For more information, the Henry Doubleday Research Association provides a whole host of facts and tips on growing organic food on their website www.hdra.org.uk, so check it out.

Getting rid of garden chemicals

If possible, it's a good idea to reduce the amount of chemicals you use in and on your garden. Many of the chemicals people use in their gardens can be harmful to the environment if they're not disposed of correctly. These include pesticides, herbicides and fertilisers.

These chemicals should not be poured into drains, sinks or toilets as this causes pollution of the water system, particularly if large quantities are disposed of.

As well as killing insect pests, many pesticides are also toxic to pets and wildlife and will contain warnings on the packaging, including recommendations for how to dispose of them safely. If there are no guidelines for disposal, don't assume they are safe. You should contact the manufacturer directly for further advice.

Always store garden chemicals in their original packaging so their usage instructions are readily to hand. Existing quantities should be used up completely wherever possible. Because of the chemical residue they take up, empty garden chemical containers can't be recycled.

Don't be a water waster

Saving water applies as much to our gardens as it does to our homes.

Our gardens need water most when it's summer, which is why you'll often see a whole neighbourhood out with their watering cans, sprinklers and hoses merrily dousing their gardens with water. Most people tend to use tap water – this has come from our rivers, streams or aquifers, which are underground rocks that supply rivers, streams and wetlands with water throughout the year.

If you look at the knock-on effect our wasting water can have, not just on the environment, but on our purses, a shortage of water means we're having to pay more and more for it. Water companies pass on the costs of treating water to their customers either through metering your water supply or through standing charges. So, excessive watering in the garden is costing you!

There are quite a few simple tricks to save water in your garden.

Top water-saving tips

- Recycle water from your home and use it in the garden.
- Improve soil structure and use materials to keep moisture where it's needed most.
- Use various irrigation systems instead of hoses or sprinklers.
- Grow drought-tolerant plants rather than thirsty ones.

Choose drought-resistant plants

All plants need watering, but some are more resistant to drought and can cope without watering during short dry spells. Choose plants that are naturally more tolerant to dry soil such as lavenders, santolina and stachys. Drought-resistant plants, such as cistus, are also especially good for sandy soils.

Keeping the moisture in

Add plenty of organic matter to your soil before planting – this will help the soil to retain moisture, enabling the roots of young plants to thrive. This is yet another good reason to get composting.

Another way of keeping the moisture in your soil is to apply a mulch of compost, bark chips or cocoa shells to the surface of the soil. Mulches also help to keep weeds in check.

The best time to apply a mulch is spring, but you can add them at any time as long as the soil is damp. Large containers can also be topped off with a mulch of bark or gravel so you don't have to water them so often.

Hanging baskets

Hanging baskets dry out very quickly, which is why, when you get around to watering them, water tends to pour through the bottom. That's because really dry compost doesn't soak up water very well. Try to buy hanging baskets with built-in reservoirs, or add water-retaining granules, to give roots a chance to benefit from watering rather than having it all run away through the bottom.

Water in the evening

The best time to water your garden or plants is in the evening, so that moisture doesn't immediately evaporate in the heat of the sun. Watering at dusk will give your plants a chance for a long overnight drink. An automatic watering system, which uses a timer on a tap, can be set to come on at any time, even when you're away. Water seeps out of small holes in pipes, delivering water to where it is most needed, making these a good investment.

Grey water

'Grey water' (water that has already been used for washing or bathing) can be recycled for use in the garden.

You can siphon off bath water into buckets using a hose – but this is pretty time-consuming and backbreaking. An easier alternative is to buy a diverter, which allows bath and shower water to be diverted to hose pipes or storage butts.

Washing machines can also be fitted with diverters that directly empty all water into a pipe or bucket.

There are a few golden rules with grey-water recycling:

- Never reuse water that contains strong detergents, chemicals or household cleaning agents.
- Never drink grey water and do not use it on edible produce such as fruit and vegetables.
- Never reuse bathing water when a family member is ill or using a topical skin treatment.
- Do not repeatedly water the same spot with grey water; spread it around the garden instead.
- Always store grey water separately from other water supplies.
- Do not store grey water for long periods of time, as it will go stagnant.
- Ensure you protect your mains water against contamination by backflow (in order to comply with the Water Supply Regulations 1999).

Water butts

If you collect rainwater or grey water, you will often have more than you can use at once, and this is where water butts come in useful. But remember to store rainwater and grey water in separate butts.

Collecting water from roofs or any flat surface is a great way to save water for use outdoors. You can either get a single water butt or you can link several together to collect water during rainy periods. A water butt can provide enough water for the entire garden during dry spells and they come in a range of sizes. Make sure you get one with a well-fitting cover to stop debris such as leaves from falling in. Some also come with a child-safety lid. You can buy water butts from garden centres and large DIY stores.

If we all used water butts, we could help to avoid local flooding. When we experience a heavy rainfall, the run-off from roofs, roads, pavements and other nonporous surfaces means that a torrent of water is sent to drains. When the system can't cope, you can get flooding. When you're planning hard surfacing in your garden, or redoing your drive, consider using a porous surface to do your bit to reduce local flooding.

Get the composting habit

Making compost is a bit like making a cake – you need the right ingredients, the correct temperature and moisture.

You'll need to feed your compost a good mix of 'activators' and 'bulkers'. Activators rot quickly so will help to get the composting process going. All your fruit and vegetable peelings and uncooked fruit and veggie leftovers, weeds, young hedge clippings, crushed eggshells, tea bags and coffee grounds, dead flowers and just a dash of grass clippings are ideal activators. Bulkers cook a bit more slowly. These materials are needed to give body to the finished compost – otherwise you'll end up with a smelly, slimy mess.

To help the rotting process along, you should chop everything up beforehand. This also reduces the bulk of your compost dramatically, so you can get more in when you need to.

You can add the following to your compost:

- Fruit and vegetable scraps
- Tea bags
- Coffee grounds
- Old flowers
- Bedding plants
- Old straw and hay
- Vegetable plant remains
- Strawy manures
- Young hedge clippings
- Soft prunings
- Perennial weeds
- Gerbil, hamster and rabbit bedding
- Wood ash
- Paper towels and bags

There are also super ingredients that heat up and activate your compost:

- Comfrey leaves
- Young weeds
- Grass cuttings
- Chicken manure
- Pigeon manure

These 'ingredients' are slow to rot – only add them in small quantities:

- Autumn leaves
- Tough hedge clippings
- Woody prunings
- Sawdust
- Wood shavings
- Cardboard (tubes, egg boxes etc.)
- Plant stems
- Twigs
- Egg boxes
- Animal manures

Don't put in:

- Coal and coke ash
- Cat litter
- Dog faeces
- Disposable nappies
- Glossy magazines
- Plastic
- Glass
- Metal
- Perennial weeds such as dandelions
- Diseased plants
- Meat
- Fish
- Cooked food

First steps

If you're a bit nervous about starting composting, why not join a community composting scheme (see www.communitycompost.org). Or you could check out the Composting Association, at www.compost.org.uk.

The Henry Doubleday Research Association (HDRA) is THE place to find out in greater detail how to make the perfect compost. The National Organic Gardens in Ryton, near Coventry, is home to the HDRA and a great place to visit and be inspired to compost and grow your own. Their website contains lots of fact sheets; check them out at www.hdra.org.uk.

Composting bits and bobs
Buying your bin

Many local authorities now provide subsidised home compost bins, so they're probably your best first port of call when buying one. Or you could try any of the suppliers listed at the end of this chapter.

The Green Cone converts organic kitchen waste into 90 per cent water, oxygen and a small amount of soil conditioner, which seeps into the surrounding soil. Made from 50 per cent recycled plastic, it costs £59.99 plus £6.99 postage and packing. This might seem like an expensive option, but some local authorities offer the Green Cone, so it's worth checking. Call 0800 731 2572 or visit www.greencone.com for more information.

Where to put your bin

Compost bins don't normally have, or need, a base as free access to the soil allows good drainage. And because they're placed directly onto the earth, the worms and insects that help the composting process can get in.

However, you'll still need to put your compost bin somewhere where it's easy for you to get to — you're less likely to use it if it's in a hard to reach place.

How long does it take?

You can make compost in six to eight weeks, or it can take a year or more — it all depends on what you put in, and the conditions (heat, moisture, etc.).

When your compost is ready, all the material you've put in the bin will have turned dark brown. It should also smell slightly earthy, but it's still best if you leave it for a month or two to 'mature' before using it.

Don't worry if your compost is a bit lumpy or stringy, with bits of eggshell and twigs dotted around — it's still perfectly all right to use.

Once you're ready to use your compost, simply lift the bin up in the air (you may need two of you to do this) to expose your compost. If you've been feeding your compost a 'balanced diet', it should form a neat heap like a big sandcastle.

Any uncomposted material at the top of your 'sandcastle' should be returned to your composting bin, to start again. The composted material can be now be used on your garden.

Wriggly worms

A lot of compost converts find that using a wormery helps with their composting. A wormery is divided into a number of chambers and one of these houses a number of special worms. It's simple to use, as all you have to do is drop your daily kitchen waste, some 'roughage' in the form of cardboard egg boxes and the like, plus 'wormfood' flakes (available from your wormery provider) into the bin and forget about it. The worms feed on the food waste and convert it into concentrated liquid feed (which you can then dilute with water and use as a plant food) and bio-rich organic compost.

You can learn more about wormeries, and buy them, by visiting www.wigglywrigglers.co.uk and www.originalorganics.co.uk.

Top tips for a greener garden

● Protect delicate plants and containers against frost with a cosy cocoon of recycled bubble-wrap or straw.

● Don't throw out those old net curtains just yet – they're great for shading areas of the garden and are good for keeping carrot fly off your prize roots.

- Old car tyres make excellent planters for potatoes – stack them on top of each other as the potatoes grow.
- Fill an old pallet with compost to make a herb garden.
- Ice-lolly sticks can be recycled to make plant labels.
- Broken bits and pieces of cups, plates and the like can be used as 'crocks' at the bottom of your pots and planters, to help with drainage.
- Old kitchen foil, milk-bottle tops or old CDs can be strung together to help scare the birds away.
- Yoghurt pots make great mini-pots for seedlings – just pierce the bottoms to provide drainage.
- Cut the necks off plastic bottles to concentrate watering where you need it – this is especially good for small border plants and anything in long planters.
- If slugs are a problem, you can reuse small plastic containers as slug traps. Fill the container with beer or milk and sink it into the ground. Or if you'd rather be more humane, try scattering broken eggshells around your plants – slugs don't like slithering across those. An old piece of carpet or a sprinkling of gravel should have a similar effect. Slugs don't like coffee grounds either.
- Large plastic bottles – cut in half – make great cloches or mini-greenhouses. They keep slugs at bay, too.
- Use old cardboard egg boxes as biodegradable seed trays.
- To fill in small gaps in your lawn, sow grass seed on used tea bags and use them to fill the holes.

Growing a wildlife-friendly garden

Encourage birds into your garden – they'll help keep the pest numbers down. Create a special area in your garden for wildlife and choose plants that provide food for birds and insects.

As well as a bird table, build a butterfly table by hanging a piece of plywood from a tree branch from a length of string. Place jam-pot lids of sugar dissolved in water on top for the butterflies to sip. You can also plant buddleia (butterfly bush) and honeysuckle to encourage butterflies into your garden.

Keep a pile of logs, woody prunings and hedge clippings in a corner of the garden to encourage toads and hedgehogs, who act as natural pest controllers.

WHAT YOU CAN SAVE

Using grey water can save up to 18,000 litres of water a year for each person, which represents 33 per cent of household water use.

You can save a fortune in compost by making your own, as well as reducing the amount of household and garden waste that goes to landfill sites. If you have to use any bought compost, don't buy peat-based. Peat has to be harvested from peat bogs, which are a very precious and endangered natural environment.

TOP FIVE TIPS

1. Grow your own organic fruit and vegetables, to reduce your reliance on supermarket produce.
2. Invest in a wormery to speed up your composting and produce liquid plant feed at the same time.

3. Encourage wildlife into your garden, to feed on insect pests and slugs. Then you won't have to resort to pesticides.
4. Always dispose of garden chemicals responsibly.
5. Save 'grey water' to use on your garden, and cut down on water wastage.

USEFUL CONTACTS

The **Henry Doubleday Research Association** (www.hdra.org.uk) has plenty of information on growing organic food and making compost.

Community Composting (www.communitycompost.org) has plenty of information on getting involved in a scheme near you.

The **Composting Association** (www.compost.org.uk) has loads of helpful advice on composting.

The **Organic Gardening Catalogue** (www.organiccatalog.com) supplies a good range of compost bins.

The Bin Company (www.thebincompany.com) not only sells home composting bins, but also biodegradable bags and wormeries.

Recycle Works (www.recycleworks.co.uk) have a wide range of domestic compost bins in various styles (many are made from FSC timber), plus wormeries and shredders. Call 01254 820088 for details.

For wormeries, visit www.wigglywrigglers.co.uk or www.originalorganics. co.uk.

The **Environment Agency** produces some useful leaflets to help you save water in the home and garden. Visit www.environment-agency.gov.uk for more information.

Gardening Which? can only be purchased through subscription, but has regular features on gardening topics such as how to save water in the garden. They also publish useful fact sheets and reports on all aspects of gardening. Visit www.gwfreetrial.co.uk for a month's free trial.

8
Taking it to the next level

With energy and water costs creeping ever higher, there has never been a better time to invest in our homes to make them more energy and water efficient.

It makes sense to live as green and lean a lifestyle as you can, so here are some ideas. Adopt even a few of them and you will save money – and the environment.

Renewable energy

Using energy from renewable sources such as solar and wind power can reduce the amount of fossil fuels we use. This in turn cuts down on harmful greenhouse-gas emissions that cause climate change.

The most common methods of harnessing renewable energy to generate electricity are wind energy, hydroelectric turbines or photo-voltaic solar panels. Buying and fitting your own solar panels will give you decades of service, reduce your CO_2 emissions and cut your bills, but generating your own electricity is usually expensive. Using renewable energy to heat your home and provide you with hot water, though, is much more cost effective. For more information on eco-friendly energy, see chapter 2.

Sunny days

Photovoltaics (PVs) use sunlight to generate electricity, but they are expensive, costing an average of £10,000. However, you may be able to get a grant towards some of the installation costs.

For further information on choosing, setting up and maintaining a small-scale photovoltaic system, the Centre for Alternative Technology

(CAT) publishes a resource guide listing manufacturers, suppliers and installers (www.cat.org.uk).

Getting into hot water

Rather than attempting to generate power from the sun's rays, you can just use them to heat your water. Solar hot-water heating uses heat from the sun to provide up to 55 per cent of your domestic hot water.

There are two main types of solar water-heating panel available – flat plate and evacuated tubes. The cost of a flat-plate system, including the cost of professional installation, is from £2,000 to £5,000 with a payback period of between 5 and 7 years. Evacuated tube systems are more expensive – prices range from £3,500 to £6,000 for professional installation.

However, prices are likely to come down as the technology becomes more familiar and readily available, and quotes do vary, so it's worth shopping around to get a few estimates before you go ahead.

Once the system is up and running, it should need very little maintenance and should last for decades. All you need is an annual inspection of the panels and the system to see that everything's still working properly and that there's no corrosion or condensation.

Let it rain

We introduced in chapter 7 the benefits of collecting water to use on your garden. Several companies provide equipment to collect rainwater from the roof and store it in large tanks in the cellar. The stored water is then used to flush loos, supply the washing machine and the outside tap.

CAT also publish a 'Water Supply, Treatment and Sanitation' resource guide, which is a comprehensive directory of useful contacts, and tip sheets including 'Water Conservation in The Home' and 'Making Use of Grey Water in The Garden'.

Wood-burning stoves

Domestic wood-fired heating systems come in all shapes and sizes and can use various types of fuel, from logs to pellets. A wood-burning stove usually just heats one main room, and normally has a back boiler to heat water.

A domestic wood-burning stove will cost you around £500 to £1,000 depending on the size and model you choose. Automated boilers are more expensive, but you may be able to get a grant towards the costs of installation.

Grants

There are a number of grants available to help make your home as energy efficient as possible. For example, you could get between 40 and 50 per cent towards the cost of installing solar electricity equipment. For a domestic user this could amount to up to £400. Check the grant search scheme on the Energy Saving Trust website (www.est.org.uk) to see whether you could be eligible.

Eco-loos

These really aren't as frightening or basic as they sound! Composting toilets don't use any water, which is a big plus. Additionally, you can use the composted waste in non-food areas of the garden. Keeping urine separate from stools is key to a good composting toilet system, because otherwise things can get a bit whiffy.

There are various models available and their prices range from a few hundred to several thousand pounds. You can also buy a dual-chamber compost toilet designed to fill up over the course of a year.

However, some people just can't bear the idea of composting toilets. If this sounds like you, but you still want to make your toilet a little more environmentally friendly, for about £500 you could fit an Aquatron to the outlet of your flush toilet. This device separates solids and liquids, with stools going straight into a composting chamber and your pee being treated in either a leach field or reed bed.

Something's cooking

For an extremely energy-efficient method of cooking, why not try a hay box? Also known as a Victory Oven, this literally involves lining a box with some hay and using it to cook your food. It's particularly good for cooking stews, casseroles, soups, rice, root vegetables and porridge.

To cook using a hay box you need a heavy dish or pan with a tight-fitting lid. You'll also need to heat food first on the hob for about ten minutes to bring it to boiling point. Once it's hot, you wrap the sealed dish in a towel and sit it in the hay box – rather like a nest. It takes about four times as long to cook food in a hay box than it would in a conventional oven. How quickly the food cooks depends on the tempera-ture outside the box, so it needs to sit in a warm place. And don't leave the box anywhere that mice can get at it – they might see all that hay as a potential des-res!

Food tends to cook better if you don't overfill the dish. It's also impor-tant not to get the hay wet from either the steam or from any spilled liquid.

If you're careful, the hay can be used again and again, although you may need to add a little more as time passes, as it will tend to settle. If you're not planning to use your hay box for a while, make sure the hay in it is kept dry. Microbes can develop in wet hay, and once these undesirables are flourishing, this increases the temperature of the hay and can cause fire. That's why hay is normally stored above animals in barns!

The other added bonus of a hay box is that it's easy for you to make your own out of recycled materials you have lying around, making it a great way to reuse and recycle household waste. The Centre for Alternative Technology provides an excellent fact sheet on how to make and use a hay box.

'Green' paint

Manufacturing paint uses loads of energy. Add to that the toxicity of the paint itself and you can see why paint isn't exactly environment-friendly.

We've already seen in chapter 6 that volatile organic compounds (VOCs) can irritate the eyes, nose and throat, which is why most paints now carry a VOC rating. Try to go for the lowest possible VOC rating you can. However, some of the water-based paints low in VOCs contain even more harmful chemicals:

These include:

- Alkylphenols – these are hormone disrupters that also bioaccumulate in the body.
- Vinyl resins – some people believe these can cause lung and liver damage, and could even increase the risk of cancer.
- Titanium dioxide – often used for improved whiteness or opacity, it is harmless to use, but the amount of energy used in its manufacture is an environmental concern.

A number of paint manufacturers now specialise in 'eco' or 'natural' paints, using natural, biodegradable ingredients. Some paints even use orange peel to make them smell good enough to eat (but please DON'T as they still contain poisonous materials!).

Even if you stick only to eco-friendly paints, it may still be worth asking for a list of ingredients. Some 'natural' paints still contain synthetic alkyds, white spirit, vinyl resins and titanium oxide, which you may not want to use.

Natural paints often cost more than conventional paints, but the hidden costs to your health and to the wider world will be much less.

If you really can't afford a natural paint, then try to use up cast-offs that would otherwise go to waste. At the very least, try to make sure that any spare paint you have lying around goes to someone who needs it and will use it (see chapter 6 for information on finding a home for your left-over paint).

Greening your whole house

Install as much insulation as you can in the roof and make sure draughts are minimised. If you have a cellar you should insulate under your floors – up to 25% of heat can be lost in this way. And check that skirtings, windows and doors are draught-proofed. It's becoming easier and more common for people to source eco-alternatives to substances like fibreglass for insulation. These include Warmcel (www.excelfibre.com) or insulation made from sheep's wool that you can get from Second Nature (www.secondnatureuk.com); for external wall insulation contact Sto (www.sto.co.uk).

Consider installing a solar hot-water heating system. These are getting cheaper all the time and only basic plumbing skills are needed for most installations.

Install efficient heat-recovery fan units in wet areas to cut down on humidity and rapid air-cooling.

Switch to a green electricity supplier – you may not even have to change your current supplier. Give them a call to see what's on offer.

Next time you buy a light bulb, make it a low-energy one – and scoop savings of up to £50 over the life of an eco-bulb.

Instead of daubing your walls in petrochemical-based paints, try more natural alternatives that are kinder to the environment. They can look fantastic too.

Use natural waxes on floors – you'll love the wholesome smell.

Buy second-hand furniture and repair it rather than buying brand new.

When building cupboards or shelving look for sources of reclaimed timber. It's often of superior quality and very competitively priced – and it has none of the brassiness of younger wood.

When purchasing any product, think about what they're made of and where they come from – the more natural the better, and the more locally they are sourced the less transport needed.

Compost your kitchen and garden waste and improve your soil for free, while reducing the waste you send to landfill.

TOP FIVE TIPS

1. Get your whole family involved in making green lifestyle choices.
2. Before you buy anything, stop to ask yourself if you could do without it – that's really the 'greenest' choice you can make. If you really can't do without, then try to buy 'green' and ethical goods.
3. Cut down your energy use as much as you can, and use 'green technology' for things like heating, insulation and plumbing.
4. Recycle absolutely everything you can.
5. Count the cost of 'convenience' to see if it's a false economy. Often the only thing you save is time, while your health and the environment could suffer.

USEFUL CONTACTS

The **Centre for Alternative Technology** (www.cat.org.uk) has advice on all aspects of 'green' technology, so check out their website or telephone 01654 705950 (email: info@cat.org.uk).

Elemental Solutions (www.elementalsolutions.co.uk) has environmentally friendly toilets.

For environment-friendly paints, visit the **Green Shop** (www.greenshop. co.uk).

Excel Fibre (www.excelfibre.com) supplies Warmcel insulation.

Second Nature (www.secondnatureuk.com) produces insulation made from sheep's wool.

Try Sto (www.sto.co.uk) for external wall insulation.

9
Putting it all together

The truth is, generally the only thing stopping us from wasting less is the fact that we're creatures of habit and, despite knowing the benefits of changing our behaviour, breaking a habit is never easy.

Some of the changes outlined in this book do require a bit of effort and they almost certainly require you to think in a different way.

The ideas we've shared with you are, of course, only suggestions, but the possibilities are limitless and it's up to you whether you just dip your toe in the water, or take things to their greenest level.

It won't be practical to do everything immediately. The aim of this book is to help you to think in a different way, so you can reap the benefits of a healthier, happier and wealthier life. The rest, as they say, is up to you.

> If you are going to make the lifestyle changes outlined in this book then you need to change the way you think about things generally. Caring about the environment doesn't just have to be a 'do-gooder's' ethos; it can also highlight the smaller things that really matter to you – things for your own selfish needs.

Getting a life balance

We all make choices. For example, if you have to work late you're not going to be able to go out for dinner with your friends. Sometimes that's just unavoidable. But if it's become habitual, then you really do need to stop and think about your main concerns and how you are managing your time.

The best way to cope with all the competing priorities you have to deal with on a daily basis is to get some sort of balance in your life. You need to take stock; evaluate what's important in your life and then make some hard choices. Rather like de-cluttering our homes, making 'life choices' isn't easy. It often involves letting go of things (or people). There are no right or wrong choices, either – but sometimes we need to be a bit selfish and that can make us feel guilty. However, everything has its price and only you can decide what's worth paying for and whether or not the price is right for you.

Keeping the spontaneity

For some of you, the mere idea of marking out your life like this will sap your will to live! 'What about spontaneity?' you'll cry. Well, planning your time doesn't necessarily mean you can't be spontaneous. However, it's the spontaneous acts that cause us to make lazy choices around the home that cause problems. 'I'll just throw this wine bottle in the bin, no time to recycle,' or, 'I'm going to open another!' spring to mind.

If we keep acting 'spontaneously' like this without planning our future, we're going to ruin the planet. The trick to embracing plans is to make sure that you block out a set amount of time and then use it in a creative way. If you decide you fancy a night out, make sure you have the time available and decide exactly *what* to do at the last minute.

When was the last time?
- You and your partner enjoyed a meal out together?
- You sat and played a board game with the family?
- You read a book to the end?
- You spent some free time with your best friend?

>>

- You went for a walk with the whole family?
- You found time to make contact with an old friend?
- You spent time on a hobby?

If these are 'never' events or too far in the distance for you to remember, perhaps it's time to make them happen.

Life's little rituals

The faster our pace of life becomes, the less time we seem to be spending with our friends and families. Reintroducing some of life's little rituals back into your routine can help improve your personal relationships and lead to happier and more fulfilling lives.

These are all sorts of rituals that help us to slow down and allow us to take time out from our hectic schedules. They are especially rewarding, because they allow us to deepen our relationships with one another. Just think how much more enjoyable mealtimes would be if they were less frantic and you didn't have to compete with the TV to get your partner's attention. Or you could follow a meal with a games evening for the family.

You can also create home rituals for yourself. Why not sit down to a favourite film or look through old photo albums? You could also consider taking up a hobby you enjoy. Or you could block off some time for a 'home spa' and give yourself some relaxing beauty treatments.

Nostalgia

When you think back to your own childhood, was there anything that your parents or grandparents did around the home that you enjoyed as a child and that you could do for your own children? You could make a ritual of decorating the home for a special occasion or religious festival. Or why not get together with some neighbours and organise a street party?

Lighten the load

Despite surrounding ourselves with a range of expensive labour-saving devices, we're spending more time than ever before on household chores. The average British family now washes five loads a week, which uses huge amounts of energy, water and detergent. This harms the environment and saps our cash and time.

Do you remember that your granny used to have a 'wash day'? And she never seemed to be stressed and rushing around the way that we do. For example, even though our washing machines and tumble dryers mean we can do a lot more laundry a lot more quickly, we just do more and more of it.

More women work these days (unlike Granny), yet still it is women who do most of the household chores. Sharing these chores with the family will ease the burden on poor old Mum.

Why not draw up a list of chores that need to be done and mark on there who is responsible for what? You could even link it to the kids' pocket money.

The list will also act as a useful time audit, so when you look at it you can ask yourself whether it really is necessary to do eight loads of washing a week!

Old habits die hard

One of the aims of this book is to convince you that you need to change some of your habits. However, change can also be quite stressful and while the end result may be beneficial, the process could be pretty traumatic for some of you.

A lot of the things you need to do to cut down on your waste means casting off some emotional and habitual baggage that you may have carried with you since childhood, and starting to look at things in a new way. You may look back and remember how your own parents dealt with household waste, for instance. Did that influence the way you think about what you waste and what you throw away? How many times can you remember your parents saying to you, 'Isn't it about time you got rid of that old thing?' or 'Chuck that out. It's no good. It's rubbish.' If you've been brought up to behave in a certain way and to believe certain things, then changing what you know and what you're used to doing can be extremely difficult.

Don't be too hard on yourself if you're finding some of this difficult to deal with – start small and make a few simple changes. Soon you will be able to appreciate the bigger picture and, ultimately, start thinking more about the planet as well as saving time and money. The more you experiment by making a few small changes, the more confidence you will have to carry on and try new things.

Remember the saying, 'Old habits die hard'? Well, many psychologists believe it takes between three and six months for new behaviour to become a habit. Therefore, relapses could be on the cards. For example, you may find yourself so busy at work one week that you grab those ready-meals in their wasteful packaging and, hey presto – your bins are full to overflowing again. At this point, it can be hard to pick yourself up again but, whatever you do, please don't think you're a failure, and please don't give up. It's at times like these that you need to realise how important it is to carry on and not throw in the towel. Your actions, however small (or sporadic) they may be, really do make a difference.

Choose happiness

As Abraham Lincoln once said, most people, most of the time, can choose how stressed or happy, how troubled or relaxed they want to be. So, choose to be happy!

Watch less TV

● Watching excessive amounts of TV can be bad for our health – especially for our children. There's more childhood obesity than ever before, which increases the risk of them developing heart disease and diabetes in later life. Instead of letting the children slouch on the sofa staring at the gogglebox, encourage them to swim, dance, play sports or read. As well as reducing their expectations with regard to whatever the latest craze happens to be, they will be much healthier.

Wise time

● Plan your time wisely. But make sure you set aside time in your planner to be selfish and to do what you want to do, when you want to do it. If you feel like being spontaneous – go for it!

● Use your time wisely. Eat when you're hungry, nap when you need it. Don't let the pace of life dictate how you use your time. If you want to enjoy a more leisurely feast, then plan a family meal, a dinner party, or have a clothes or book 'swap party' with some friends – get them to bring along some food to share the cost and preparation time.

● Show your love! Let your family and friends know that you value them, by making time for them.

● Use your body as it was designed to be used. Walk and run, stretch, throw things, and lift things. Dance! Sing! Jump about and generally have a blast! Exercise is good, but making love with your partner is great! Making fairy cakes with the kids, cuddling your best mate, laughing with your friends and generally having a good time are brilliant stress busters. You've got a body, so use it! It can either be a source of pleasure and fun, or a source of aches and pains.

● Avoid toxins – and not just the chemical sort! People can also be poisonous. Give all the energy vampires and negative creepy people the elbow.

TOP FIVE TIPS

1. Try not to make promises you can't keep. It's too easy to be harassed and you could find yourself giving in to every demand made on your time. Learn to say 'no' and mean it.

2. Learn something new, every day. To be happy, most of us must also be growing, expanding, learning and challenging ourselves. Read, listen, adapt and stretch to accommodate new ideas and new information.

3. Make time to eat meals together. Nowadays we tend to spend an average of twenty minutes cooking a meal and ten minutes

scoffing it down. What sort of conversation can you have with someone in ten minutes?

4. Consider paying the children for helping with extra chores. Apart from freeing up your time, this allows your children to gain some extra money, which they can put towards something they want, and will make them less reliant on you for treats.

5. Write a list of things you would like to achieve in the next five years and work towards them.

INDEX